JAVA BEANS
FOR REAL PROGRAMMERS

University of Hertfordshire

Learning and Information Services

JAVA BEANS
FOR REAL PROGRAMMERS

Peter Wayner

AP Professional

AP Professional is a Division of Academic Press

San Diego   London   Boston
New York   Sydney   Tokyo   Toronto

AP PROFESSIONAL
An Imprint of ACADEMIC PRESS
A Division of HARCOURT BRACE & COMPANY

This book is printed on acid-free paper. ∞
Copyright © 1998 by Academic Press

ACADEMIC PRESS
525 B Street, Suite 1900, San Diego, CA 92101-4495, USA
1300 Boylston Street, Chestnut Hill, MA 02167, USA
http://www.apnet.com

United Kingdom Edition published by
ACADEMIC PRESS LIMITED
24-28 Oval Road, London NW1 7DX, UK
http://www.hbuk.co.uk/ao/

Library of Congress Cataloging-in-Publication Data
Wayner, Peter
    Java Beans for Real Programmers / Peter Wayner
        p. cm.
    ISBN 0-12-738670-X
    1. Java (Computer program language) 2. JavaBeans I. Title
QA76.73.J38W393 1998
005.13'3—dc21   98-6366
                                                                              CIP

Printed in the United States of America
98 99 00 01 02 CP 9 8 7 6 5 4 3 2 1

Contents

Preface   ix

Book Notes   xi

1 Introduction   1
   The Life Sun Imagines for a Bean   3
   Adding Buzzwords to Java   5
   How Old Buzzwords Affect the New   11
   New Parts of Java Beans   14
   Conclusions   17

2 First Look   19
   The Main Applet, `Applet1`   20
   Passing Events with `NewLightEvent`   25
   A New Bean Called `StopLightPanel`   28
   Parsing the Events   35
   Conclusion   36

3 Fitting In   39
   Design Signatures   40
   Property Access   42
   Bound Properties   45
   Two-Way Bound Property (Vetoable)   49
   Event Names   52
   Conclusion   53

4 Persistence   55
Advantages and Disadvantages 56
Building in Persistence 57
Object Validation 66
Software Upgrades and Versions of Beans 68
Making Classes `Externalizable` 71
How Beans Are Serialized 72
Conclusion 72

5 Events   75
Basic Events 78
Event Listeners 79
Registering Event Listeners 82
Unicast versus Multicast Events 84
Event Adapters 85
Vetoable Events 86
Conclusion 86

6 International Beans   89
`Locale` and How to Use It 91
Creating Your Own `ResourceBundle` 94
`Format` for Different Languages 101
Date Classes for Formatting Time 107
Conclusion 107

7 Using BeanInfo   109
`BeanInfo` Interface 110
The `Introspection` Class 119
Building Your Own BeanInfo 121
Core Reflection 130
The `Method` Class 143
Using Core Reflection 144
Conclusions 145

8 BeanBoxes and Meta-Tools   147
Using BeanBox 148
Customizing Classes 152
JAR Files 160

Conclusion 160

9 An Example in Stereo   163
The `NeighborClock` Panel 164
The `Volume1` Panel 165
The `SoundMasterApplet` Demo Applet 167

10 Indicator Event Example   169
The `NumBean` Label 170
The `ThermBean` Panel 171
The `WarnBean` Panel 173
The `WarnEvent` Event 175
The `WarnAdaptor` Event Adapter 175
The `AdaptApplet` Master Applet 176

11 Self-Scrambling Example   179
The `ScramApplet` for Example 179
The `ScramBean` 180

12 A Big Event Example   183
The `TreeApp` Applet 184
The `AlphaBeatEvent` Event 187
The `BetaBeatEvent` Event 188
The `BoingPanel1` Panel 189
The `CartPanel1` Panel 192
The `DogPanel1` Panel 195
The `TriPanel1` Panel 197

13 Digging Deep   201
The `CountPanel` Panel 201
The Main Applet, `TestMD1` 202
The Output 204

Preface

I should not take complete credit for this book. I relied heavily upon sources at Sun Microcomputing and on the Net for guidance and they helped shape the book and fill in details. The documentation about Java Beans from Sun formed the foundation.

The team of people at AP Professional were incredibly gracious with their time and encouragement. I'm glad for all of their support through this manuscript. They are: Chuck Glaser, Tom Stone, Tom Park, Kira Glass, Bettina Burch, Julie Champagne, and Tom Ryan. Also, Jeff Pepper and Mike Williams helped start the book moving when they worked at AP Professional.

There were others who helped in the world beyond the text. The staff at Tax Analysts was kind enough to coordinate my consulting schedule with the demands of putting out a book. Anyone would be lucky to work for a company that was so understanding. My editors at *BYTE* and the *New York Times* have been very willing to bend their schedules around the needs of producing this book.

Finally, I want to thank everyone in my family for everything they've given through all of my life.

Peter Wayner, Baltimore, MD, October 1997
pcw@access.digex.com
http://access.digex.net:/~pcw/pcwpage.html

Book Notes

The copy for this book was typeset using the LATEX typesetting software. Several important breaks were made with standard conventions in order to remove some ambiguities. The period mark is normally included inside the quotation marks like this: "That's my answer. No. Period." This can cause ambiguities when computer terms are included in quotation marks because computers often use periods to convey some meaning. For this reason, my electronic mail address is "pcw@access.digex.com". Almost all periods are left outside the quotation marks to prevent confusion.

Chapter 1

Introduction

In the beginning there was Java. It was a simple language that offered all of the most important buzzwords: object-oriented, platform-independent, garbage collecting, multi-threaded, secure, strongly typed, etc. The language was originally designed to provide software to television set top boxes and small portable machines, but it quickly found a niche in the World Wide Web and the browser world. Today, all major Web browsers support Java applets as a way to distribute small, independent programs that run locally.

Java was a good match for the Web. It made it quite easy to create small programs to animate items on the screen or add flexible local widgets that would respond to mouse clicks. The object-oriented nature of the language helps a small applet arrive at the browser and link up successfully with larger libraries of code designed to handle drawing windows or perform other tasks. The platform independence meant that the small byte codes produce by a Java compiler could run successfully on many machines made by different companies. Today, the success of the language is obvious.

But there were still limitations to Java. Although there were many parts of the language that were fully developed and well thought out, anyone who used the language did not have access to the best tools for developing programs. Systems like Visual Basic, Borland's Delphi, and OpenDoc made it easy to create flexible program components that worked well with each other and were somewhat portable.

So, Sun moved to create Java Beans. This is a set of extensions to the Java world that would make it easier to create objects that traveled with both code and data. They could be bundled together to make an application or even inserted into a document.

The objects, known as *Beans*, could be controls like a button or a slider. Or they could be larger, more complete items like a spreadsheet or some data graphing application. They could also be faceless data processing programs that might mind the Web or convert data by encrypting it.

Once the Beans exist, anyone can use them in a flexible way. An application developer might glue together several Beans to make a quick application that would graph information about the stock price. A network watching Bean would periodically fetch the stock price from some service (`www.quote.com`, for instance); a data storage Bean would keep track of the last set of prices and feed the information to a graphing Bean. This sort of reusability is the goal of the Java Beans project.

Beans could also be bundled into documents. Technology like Corba or OpenDoc was meant to replace application-centric programming with document-centric programing. So if you write a document that needs a graph, you could insert the graphing Bean to do the work. If people wanted to edit the document, they could simply edit the data being fed to the graphing Bean. They didn't need to worry about having the proper graphing software because it traveled with the document as a Bean.

These are big goals for any language development project. They aim at taking Java and bringing it from a simple development language to a full-fledged environment that programmers can use for all of their needs.

Here is the definition that Sun offered in 1996 to the Java One conference when it announced its plans for Java Beans:

> A Bean is a reusable software component that can be manipulated visually in a builder tool.

In the time that passed, Sun softened its stance a bit. There are now invisible Beans that can't be manipulated visually because they

never draw anything on the screen.[1] Some Beans are not as reusable
as others because they've had some of their customizability stripped
out to save space and conserve bandwidth. But the spirit is still
there.

A crucial part is the builder tool. This is an editor that can
reach inside a Bean and discover the parts that can be modified or
customized. Then it presents these options to users and lets them
have their way with it.

The Java Beans technology is really about standardizing the way
we write classes. If everyone creates Java classes in the same way,
then an automated tool can be designed that will allow us to edit
the classes.

The Life Sun Imagines for a Bean

Sun has great dreams for Java Beans. It now encourages everyone to
write to the Java Beans API instead of simply writing Java programs.
This will increase reusability and make it possible for a more organic
economy in Beans to develop. There is already a good market for
Visual Basic components and C++ libraries. There is no reason why
a similar market in Beans will not emerge.

The life of a Bean is fairly simple, but it could be quite long.
In the beginning, the programmer starts with a raw class file and a
dream for a component that will help someone build applications in
the future. This component may be a control like a fancy slider or
it could be some sort of display with a fancy graph. In some cases,
the Bean might even be something invisible that will process data in
the background. There could be a whole class of Net minding Beans
in the future.

When the programmer lays out the Bean, he must choose the
API that the Bean will use to connect with the outside world. This
includes defining the methods to which the Bean will react. This is
where Java Bean programming is different from simple Java programming. A Java programmer can pretty much name the methods with

---

[1]The strength of this statement depends upon your definition of manipulating
something "visually". Some invisible Beans can be manipulated with an editing
tool that lets you change some properties.

any name under the sun. It's quite permissible to use the method `Buttinski43SkiDoo` to change the font. The code may not be that readable, but it will compile and run.

Java Beans is a more rigorous collection of rules about creating a class. That means the programmer has less flexibility in setting the names of the methods. Some can be arbitrary, but the ones for changing the parameters of a class must begin with a prefix like `set`. The Beans technology uses these rules to automate the process of modifying the Bean. If the programmer doesn't follow the rules, then someone generally can't use the Bean technology.[2]

For the most part, it takes little extra effort to write a Java Bean than a regular Java class. You get a little less flexibilty, but the rest is pretty much the same. It's up to you to get the instruction sequence complete and there is not much different about doing this with Beans.

Of course, a Java Bean programmer may want to work longer and harder at making the Bean easier to customize. Beans are meant to be reused again and again. A good Bean includes many extra methods for changing the look and detail. So a Bean programmer may spend more time adding these methods. Of course, embellishing a Bean with plenty of customizable features is not a requirement. Many programmers may whip off simple Beans that just do the job.

When the Bean is done being created, it takes on a new life. In many cases, the programmer may immediately incorporate it into a larger application. This is often the goal when people write special Beans from scratch.

In many other cases, however, the Bean may take its place in a collection that will be used again and again by different programmers in different applications. When a Bean is taken from this collection, its life follows a path that might seem different to some programmers.

---

[2]The Beans API includes the flexibility to break the rules if you need to do so. A large part of this book revolves around the `BeanInfo` data structure, which describes the basic methods, variables, and parameters used by a Bean. If you follow the rules, then the built-in Java tool will automatically construct a `BeanInfo` structure. If you don't follow the rules, you can create one yourself. It isn't a good idea to break the rules simply because someone said a foolish consistency is a hobgoblin of little minds. The rules also make the code much more readable for everyone.

The collection, after all, is a collection of Bean creation software. A Bean is taken from it by running the software to create a new object, a Bean.

This new Bean becomes a persistent object that is then bound up in an applet, an application, or a document. It carries with it the parameters and code it needs to do the job and it may never see its home again.

When the Bean is in use, a programmer can modify it. This would include calling all of the different methods built into the Bean to customize it. The changes affect the parameters bound into the Bean and they are carried with the Bean until they are changed again.

This process is quite different from the other programming systems on the market. In design environments like Visual C++ or PowerPlant, the programmer modifies a separate file of specifications. When the design is finished, a button is pushed and C code emerges. This code must be compiled before it is run.

Adding Buzzwords to Java

Every computer system is made up of buzzwords and sweat. Sun's Java development team has added both to Java to make Java Beans. You don't need to go through the sweat of building the system, but you need to understand the buzzwords to comprehend what Sun aims to do with Java Beans. The buzzwords encapsulate the ideas that Sun wants to add to the way that we program Java.

Here are some of the most important Java Beans buzzwords:

Granularity Java's basic class structure is already fairly granular. Many Java programs have already reused classes with different programs and done so with little or no modification. Java Beans are meant to be even more granular.

At first glance, this sounds something like hype. If granularity refers to reusing a bit of code in different instances, then the subroutine or function call is one of the oldest forms of granularity. How can you be more granular? Code is either reusable or it isn't. Right?

In this case, Java Beans aim to be more granular by being easier to reuse. Every time I've reused a Java class I've written, I've kept the source code near by. The basic Java AWT (Abstract Windowing Toolkit) classes are meant to be extensively reused, but if you want to change the functionality you need to subclass them and do the work yourself. Java Beans are intended to travel as objects without source code. If you want to modify parts of them, then you can do so with a well-defined interface.

For instance, a graphing Bean might have one call that would allow you to set the font used in the labels. Although this sort of functionality could have been built by a good Java class programmer, Java Beans makes it easier by encouraging this sort of behavior. It provides a structure for adding this feature that makes it easier for the objects to travel and be reused.

Introspection If a Bean is going to be flexible and travel without its source code, there must be some way to discover what makes it tick and how to modify it. The term *introspection* means that there is a standard way to extract information about a Bean from the Bean itself.

That is, there is a standard set of function calls or methods that you can invoke that will spill the Beans, so to speak, about the Bean's API. It will specify what modifications you can make and what function calls there are available. This feature forces the Bean to carry the documentation to the API with it.

This introspection is enforced by embracing a standard set of method names that are easier to understand. Functions or methods for changing some parameter or feature begin with the prefix *set*, like `setFont`.

The information from introspection emerges in a data structure from the class `BeanInfo`. This is described in Chapter 7.

Core Reflection The process of *core reflection* is the low level of the *introspection* API. That is, the core of the Bean is made visible by reflecting the most important parts to the outside person asking about it.

The reason there are two terms is that Java breaks up the process into two parts. The Core Reflection API can examine a class file and determine which parts of the class file can be modified and which methods will modify them. The Introspection API bundles this information together into a relatively coherent data structure (`BeanInfo`) that other software tools can use.

In practice, the two buzzwords end up meaning the same thing to the high-level user who is simply interested in what can be done to a particular Bean. Lower level programmers will want to understand the subtle differences if they're creating Beans that work well with the introspection and core reflection process.

Customization To a large extent the amount of customization available in a Bean depends upon the programmer. Although the Java Beans system encourages the programmer to create a Bean that is easy to customize, there is little it can do to enforce this.

Perhaps the introspection will encourage programmers to create Beans with a rich set of functions because the programmer knows that others will be able to come along and see the features that are available.

Events If the Beans are meant to be small, granular programs that will become part of larger programs, then there needs to be an easy way for Beans to communicate with each other. The event model supplied with Java Beans sets out a fairly simple structure for how events should be created and interpreted. It is up to programmers to make sure that their Bean responds correctly to the events.

Of course, there is also a standard way to use introspection to discover the events that drive a particular Bean.

To a large extent, the events used by Java Beans are quite similar to AppleEvents used by the MacOS. Each Bean must be able to respond to a set of basic events, and it can also register sets of special events with the OS to make sure that they're delivered correctly.

The Beans event model is much lower level. In a sense, all of the Beans are just libraries of code that are dynamically linked when the code is run. This allows the events to be delivered directly instead of passing through a complicated layer of the OS like AppleEvents.

Properties This a fancy name for a variable that can be accessed from outside the Bean. That is, something that can be *customized* by a programmer after the process of *introspection* reveals that it exists.

Properties are usually changed with methods that begin with prefixes like `get` and `set`.

Property Editors Many properties are easy to change. They're simply numbers or words. Others, however, have such a rich structure that it makes sense to provide a simple editing environment that is customized to them.

Java Beans provides a way for a programmer to include a customized property editor for specific properties. For instance, imagine a chess display Bean that would make it possible for someone to ship around visual chessboards. Someone writing a book on chess might include these to illustrate positions. A simple property editor would allow the Bean customizer to put pieces on the board in any fashion. The position of the pieces would be a property of the board that you would change. A better one would limit the position to conform to the rules of the game. There could only be, for instance, two bishops per side and they would travel on opposite-colored squares.

Design Signatures This term refers to the pattern used to name items inside a Java Bean. You should, for instance, name all methods that modify a property with names that begin with the prefix `set`. These guidelines are fairly strict because they are what allow the Bean technology to discover automatically much of the details about a Bean. If you don't choose the names correctly, then the Bean's features and functions cannot be found automatically.

Design Patterns Another name for design signatures.

Persistence If Beans are going to travel about, they're going to need to remember their settings. This term means that if you *customize* the *properties* of a Bean, then they'll stay *customized* as the Bean moves about.

At first glance, this doesn't sound particularly revolutionary. Many applications programs already create preferences files that keep track of the customizable parameters of the program. Beans merely carry their preferences files with them.

But the more radical effect of this is found during programming. If you're a programmer knitting together several different Beans into an application for shipping, then you're going to rely upon persistence to carry your commands. You might, for instance, set the font of a Bean during the design process. The persistence ensures that this will be carried on as people make copies of your collection of Beans.

This is a big departure from the previous component architectures. In systems like Visual C++, you would customize the components and then this information would be compiled into source code that would then be compiled into machine code. There could be only one generation of component changes.

Java Beans, however, could keep on changing and changing. Once the Beans are loosed upon the Net, anyone can use the process of *introspection* to discover how to *customize* the *properties.* This resuability could go on forever. In practice, the reusability drops with time because programmers often strip out much of the extra customizability to save space after the customization is done.

Serializable The process of making a Bean "persist" is also known as *serializing* it. This term is a bit confusing because it is also used in the context of interpreting how threads interact. In this case, the Bean documentation describes it as the process of taking all of the various properties and internal variables of the Bean and writing them to disk. That is, taking a tree-like collection of objects and writing them down in a single flat file. The notion of thread serialization doesn't apply at all in this context.

Design Time A Bean can have two different lives. At design time, the Bean is able to open itself up to someone and make all of its elements customizable. All of the mechanisms for modification are available.

Run Time After a Bean is customized, most users will only want to watch it do its stuff. In an ideal world with infinitely fast networks and infinitely big disk drives, all of the equipment and code for customizing a Bean could travel along with it. In reality, this code takes up space and bandwidth. The Java Beans standard provides a coherent way to strip away the extra customizability of a Bean and turn it into a run-time object.

Internationalization Many software packages today were designed to be easily changed to adapt to other languages and situations around the world. The customizable aspect of Java Beans makes internationalization easy to achieve.

The Beans take this to another level. Properties, methods, and events may have names that differ from country to country. One person changing a property of a Bean in France may use a different name for the property than a person in England.

This process may be quite confusing for some and many programmers will probably simply use English.

JAR Files You keep Beans in a jar, right? The puns will never end. JAR files are ZIP files that anyone can use to bundle together a boatload of classes, resource files, or whatever. The TCP/IP and HTTP protocols are inefficient when they must carry many small files. Putting them together into one bigger file makes the disk management easier and the file transfer significantly quicker.

These are some of the major buzzwords that define the Java
Beans environment. As you can see, the whole point of Java Beans is
to make it easy to create flexible components that are easy to modify.
A good collection of components will make it easy for people to bind
them together into custom applications.

How Old Buzzwords Affect the New

The Java Beans collection of buzzwords is well integrated with the
old collection of buzzwords and properties that were built into Java.
The Beans concept is meant as an additional layer on top of the old
Java structure. It relies upon many of the old features to implement
the new.

Classes The most important foundation is the Java class structure.
Beans are just more elaborate classes. They are just classes
with the right structure that makes it easy to do introspection
and customization.

Although many people will think of Beans as the most important level of granularity, they will still continue to be just new
classes underneath. The class and object model used as the
foundation for Java will still define how Beans interact. In fact,
you'll be able to subclass Beans and inherit information from a
superclass. There won't be multiple inheritance, but you'll be
able to use a simpler notion of *implementation* to provide the
same effects.

This class structure is essentially a recognition of the success
of Java to this day. A great deal of effort has been put into
creating Java interpreters, compilers, and byte code tools. The
standard Java class mechanism is an essential part of all of
these tools. Although it would be nice to start fresh and add
much of the Java Beans ideal to the lowest possible level, it is
far from practical.

Many programmers may continue to mix both class libraries
and Beans. The libraries will be used for simpler data specific
details, while the Beans will contain all of the visual interfaces.

To some extent, the decision on whether to use a simple class or a more sophisticated Bean will be a style decision made by the programmer. Simple data handling code doesn't need the flexibility and customizability of a full-fledged Bean. But some programmers may want to add it out of a mixture of pride and planning for the future.

Sometimes people use the term "Bean" to refer to the JAR file containing the basic Bean class and all of its additional classes and tools.

Events The Java AWT contains an event handling mechanism for shipping events to the different components in the AWT. The Java Beans Events build on top of this structure by providing a way to create a central register of who will respond to each event.

In the old AWT structure, the Events are passed along up a hierarchy of components until one of them handles the event and takes it out of the system. The AWT would use the position of the mouse and the focus to determine which component got first crack at an event.

In the Beans world, a Bean can register different types of events and specify that it should be notified when they are generated. For instance, a special stock price graphing Bean might register an event with the name `newStockPriceEvent`. When the network minding Bean detected that the price had changed, it would generate the event and pass it directly to the graphing Bean.

Methods Java classes always had methods. These methods could either be available to outside classes (*public*) or be hidden from outside classes (*private*). The Beans world provides even more control over who can access these classes. The entire process of introspection can hide some public classes and draw attention to others.

Security One of Java's greatest assets is its ability to run code in a protected section of memory. This is often called the "sandbox". This same security model is used as the foundation for

Java Beans. There are no major differences or enhancements to it. A Java Bean that is loaded into a WWW browser from the Web will still face the same security limitations as a simple applet.

The security mechanism can affect how some parts of the Bean functionality can change depending upon the environment. An applet typically runs in a very security-conscious environment that limits its access to the public methods of classes to which it has legitimate access. A Java application, on the other hand, can access all classes.

In these different environments, the process of introspection will behave differently. If an applet doesn't have legitimate access to a class's function, the Introspection calls will reveal nothing. In other environments, they will tell all.

Multithreading Java is a multithreaded environment and Beans are just Java classes. So they will run as part of multiple threads and they should be written to be threadsafe.

AWT The old Java Abstract Windowing Toolkit continues to be important to Java Beans developers. A component Bean is literally that, an object that inherits its behavior from the AWT class `Component`. The Beans can then be bundled together in applets or applications and they interact in much the same way that the old Components did in old AWT programming.

The Event model is also integrated with the AWT class of `Event`, but it has been extended with a few more capabilities.

Anyone who is familiar with AWT programming will be able to use plenty of this knowledge to do Bean programming. Anyone who isn't familiar should become familiar with it.

Each of these parts of the original Java technology is a crucial part of the foundation of Java Beans. The ideas incorporated in the Beans were intended to be simply a layer on top of the original Java. This process made it possible to add new features without destroying the previous functionality.

New Parts of Java Beans

The Java Beans introduce a number of new pieces of software and technology to the Java world. Some are very practical tools and others are more ephemeral types that mold the data manipulated.

BeanInfo

BeanInfo is a new Java interface that contains the data to describe a Bean. It is constructed by the Core Reflection and Introspection APIs when they are asked to discover the basic features of a Bean. Some of the BeanInfo can also come from a special class created by the programmer to produce information about the Bean. In this case, this information may also be mixed with the results coming from the Core Reflection API.

The data structure of BeanInfo is pretty straightforward. It lists the various properties, events, and methods built into a Bean and then groups them according to which methods affect which properties. So a property like Font is grouped with the methods for changing the Font, like getFont and setFont.

A programmer is responsible for choosing the correct names so that the Core Reflection API can assemble this information automatically. If the names don't provide enough clues, the programmer must provide another class that creates a BeanInfo object with the correct information.

The BeanInfo data structure is generally created and manipulated by editing tools like BeanBox that are actually changing the structure of a Bean. In most cases, a programmer will have little need to manipulate directly the information in the structure. Most people will rely upon tools to do the manipulation for them. In some cases, you may want to check to see if a particular class supports some method or property and then you might use the functions directly. But this will probably be the odd case, not the common one.

In some cases, a programmer may want to rely upon the BeanInfo mechanism to add some abstraction to the process. For instance, the programmer may create something to manipulate a set of arbitrary Beans coming from many different positions. It could use the

`BeanInfo` mechanism to discover which method must be called to manipulate the `foo` property. This would allow a good deal of flexibility in the data structure because old and new Beans with different `foo` manipulation methods could coexist.

Chapter 7 shows how to use the `BeanInfo` class and many of the other classes that are used to assemble the description of the Bean, such as `BeanDescriptor`, `FeatureDescriptor`, and `PropertyDescriptor`.

Customizer

The `Customizer` interface is another important part of the new set of classes provided with the Beans API. If your Bean comes with a class that implements this interface, then it provides a way for a basic user to customize a Bean without looking at the code. That is, it will provide a graphical interface to changing the basic parameters in a Bean.

The class implementing this interface should be a `Component` because it will be installed in some AWT window.

PropertyEditor

A similar interface is the `PropertyEditor`. This allows you to provide a graphical way for someone to edit one of the properties. Many of the standard types (`int`, `float`, etc.) are handled by simple editing fields, but you may want to provide a `PropertyEditor` descendant if you have special requirements. For instance, the volume may be integers between 0 and 11, not any arbitrary integer.

This is a fairly complicated class with a wide range of possibilities. If you use it well, then many basic Beans users will be able to access your Bean and modify it.

PropertyChangeListener

A `PropertyChangeEvent` is a special type of event that emerges whenever a special type of property is changed. It carries information to any other Bean informing it of the change.

You might use such an event if you wanted Beans to coordinate how they work. One Bean may ask to know if another changes a property. For instance, a numerical readout Bean may want to know if the property it is displaying is changed.

A Bean implements the `PropertyChangeListener` interface if it's going to be looking for `PropertyChangeEvents` fired by someone else.

A close cousin is the `VetoableChangeListener`, which lets the listener have some input on whether the change should be allowed. Chapter 9 shows how `VetoableChangeEvents` can be used by neighbors to agree upon how loud a stereo can go. It's a hypothetical example, but it illustrates how to process the events.

BeanBox

The BeanBox is a Bean manipulation tool distributed with the Java Bean Development Kit (BDK). It is a first-generation Bean editor and it provides much of the basic functionality. You can use the BeanBox to open up a Bean, discover its contents, and manipulate them. You can also bind several Beans together into an application.

JAR Files

JAR files are compressed archives that contain a variety of different files in one big mass. This allows the files to travel faster through the network because the browsers need to send only one request for a big file instead of many small requests for a variety of class files. The structure of TCP/IP and HTTP places plenty of overhead in starting up a request for a file.

JAR files are not limited to Java Beans—they are useful for any type of Java application. But they're fully integrated into the Bean world.

The basic structure of a JAR file is not much different from that of a .ZIP file. There is a manifest containing a list of the files that are compressed in a Bean. Public domain compression algorithms are used to compress the data and some of these are tuned to do a good job with Java byte code. A .ZIP file, on the other hand, uses a different collection of compression algorithms and some are not in the public domain.

Conclusions

The world of Java Beans is not an entirely new programming language—it's just a set of rules for doing a better job programming in Java. If you follow the rules, then your parts (known as "Beans") will be easier to circulate. In fact, automatic tools will be able to manipulate them and stitch them together. This will help both experienced and inexperienced programmers use them quickly and efficiently. The inexperienced programmers will benefit the most because they'll be able to work with deep tools developed by experienced programmers, but they'll manipulate them and change them at arm' s length.

The rules are known as "design signatures" and they're not particularly complex. You name classes and some standard methods in the same way. Most people may already adhere to these rules because they make good common sense.

The rules, though, are only half of the story. There is also a great deal of new code bundled in APIs. Some may think of this code as Java 1.1. The libraries do things like handle the "Internationalization" of code. That is, you can make the code change the words and scripts based upon where it is run.

The long-range goal is better code mobility and functionality. The success of this will depend more upon the programmer than anyone else. You can think of the Java Beans rules as the Sun programming team dragging you to water. They can't make you drink in the Beans way of life. You're free to use as much as you want. Some situations will call for you to do a great job and include plenty of functionality. Others will ask for a minimal Bean. That flexibility is still there. The rules are pretty reasonable.

Here are some of the most important lessons:

- Beans are flexible bundles of methods and data that can be stored and brought back to life.

- Beans are a different way of doing object-oriented programming. Instead of writing classes and linking them together with the compiler, you create actual versions of the objects and link them together.

- Some light users may see Beans as simple components that can be manipulated and linked together with high-level tools like a BeanBox. They may never see any of the deeper rules and structure discussed in this book. The long-range goal is to make it easy for these casual users to plug Beans together.

- In order to implement this endless linking, the programmer must follow some rules about naming parameters, variables, functions, and classes in order to make it possible for other programmers and their creations to understand the interface. These rules, often called "design signatures", are not complicated.

- The Beans API also contains techniques for creating International user interfaces that change their appearance as they move around the world.

- The Beans API is really about core reflection and introspection. That is, letting another program peer into the guts of a Bean so it can interface with it.

- There are two levels of introspection. The lowest level known as core reflection uses the `Class`, `Method`, and `Field` classes to scan the different parts of a Bean. The higher level built by the Introspector API consists of the `BeanInfo` derivatives which assemble all of the data into one huge data structure.

- Beans communicate with events. You link up the Beans by having them issue events to each other. This should be a dynamic process.

Chapter 2

First Look

The best place to begin understanding the notion of Java Beans is to look at an example. Some of the concepts may not be easy to grasp in their entirety, but the approach does guarantee that you'll be able to see the big picture. The details can wait until you read the chapters.

This example is a simple stoplight that is built on top of a basic `Canvas` from the AWT. The result should be an independent object that can be inserted into many different applications without recompiling. It should be mobile because it was written to conform with the set of rules for creating a Bean.

If you know Java well, you should be able to interpret what is happening here. The code, after all, is just basic Java that should run on any machine that runs Java. It was written, however, to follow the basic rules and this book is about explaining those rules.

This example consists of three basic classes. `Applet1` is the subclass of `Applet` that installs the Bean so you can test it. `StopLightPanel` is a class that is the Bean itself. The Bean and the Applet communicate among themselves by passing events from the `NewLightEvent` class.

This chapter will list the code for each of these three classes and then explain what is happening on a line-by-line basis. It will include pointers to other parts of the book so you can read about the concepts in more detail.

The Main Applet, `Applet1`

The name `Applet1` is not particularly revealing, but it is meant to
be fairly anonymous. The point of creating a Bean is to produce
something that can be used over and over again in different circumstances. The nature of the circumstances isn't incredibly important.
`Applet1` is just a class intended to give you an example of how the
Beans may function.

In fact, you may never need to use the lessons about how to
construct a class like `Applet1`. The end goal of the Beans world is
to create meta-tools like BeanBox that let you stitch together Beans
in a more sophisticated development environment. You may never
need to write a class like `Applet1` because these tools will do the
work for you.

There is one major difference here. The individual Beans are created with the `new` command. This is not necessarily the correct way
to do it. The Beans package comes with a new method `instantiate`
that is the better way to start up an object. It first looks on the
disk to see if there is an object of the right class that has already
been serialized. That is, one that has been written out to disk by the
`writeObject` method. If it's there, it will pull it back into existence.
If it isn't there, then it will revert to creating a new version of the
class with the `new` command.

Why didn't I use `instantiate` here? Because I wanted to be
guaranteed that a new version would emerge. I wanted to add the
links myself between the events by hand. You can think of this level
as doing the work of the BeanBox application, a program that can be
used to link Beans together graphically. (See Chapter 8.) If I used
`instantiate` in this case, I might end up with multiple instances of
the same link for passing events.

Many people who program in Beans will rarely write an bit of
code like this `Applet`. They'll create their `Component` Beans sepa-
rately and then use BeanBox to do the work of `instantiate` and
linking. Then, it will write them out to disk. This example, however, does a better job of illustrating how the guts of the Java Beans
world works than a high-level pass through the BeanBox. (Turn to
Chapter 8 for that.)

```
package stop;
import java.awt.*;
import java.awt.event.*;
import java.applet.*;
import java.util.*;
public class Applet1 extends Applet {
   StopLightPanel light1=null;
   StopLightPanel light2=null;
   Button startMeUp1=null, startMeUp2=null;
  //Initialize the applet
  public void init() {
     catch (Exception e) { e.printStackTrace(); }}
  public String startButtonName(){
    Locale l=this.getLocale();
    String answer="Start"; // The default
    String country=l.getCountry();
    String language=l.getLanguage();
        if ((country=="US") && (language=="EN")){
          answer="Start";
        } else if ((country=="GB") && (language=="EN")){
          answer="Go";
        } else if ((language=="FR")){
          answer="Commence";
        }
    return answer; }
  //Component initialization
  public void jbInit() throws Exception{
    add(startMeUp1=new Button(startButtonName()+" 1"));
    add(startMeUp2=new Button(startButtonName()+" 2"));
    add(light1=new stopLightPanel());
    add(light2=new stopLightPanel());
    light1.addNewLightEventListener(light2);
    light2.addNewLightEventListener(light1);
      }
 public boolean action(Event e, Object o){
   if (e.target==startMeUp1){
       light1.processNewLightEvent
          (new NewLightEvent (light2, NewLightEvent.Red));
   } else if (e.target==startMeUp2){
       light2.processNewLightEvent
          (new NewLightEvent (light2, NewLightEvent.Red));
   }
    return true; }
}
```

Here are the most important highlights of this class file described in the order in which they occur.

StopLightPanel light1=null There are two versions of the class
   StopLightPanel that will be added here. They will get commands from the master here, **Applet1**, as well as from each
   other.

try { jbInit(); } The normal **init** method calls a secondary
   method **jbInit** to do the work. This construction was dic-
   tated by Borland's JBuilder which was used to construct this
   example. It provides a skeleton when the applet is originally
   created and I left this idiom in place. The exception handling
   mechanism used here makes an ideal way to debug problems
   that occur. You may want to try to use this yourself in many
   other cases when you're debugging code.

startButtonName() This method will produce a **String** that contains the name that will appear in the two buttons, **startMeUp1**
   and **startMeUp2**. This string is generated by a method so it is
   International.

   This one method is a pretty lame way to handle Internationalizing an application. Chapter 6 describes how to use more
   complicated resource files and more substantial classes to do a
   good job creating a Bean that will speak to users throughout
   the world in their native language.

Locale l=this.getLocale(); The class **Locale** is found in the
   package **java.util**. It is a fairly robust data structure for
   capturing the various combinations of language and nationality
   throughout the world. Each panel (like **Applet1**) now comes
   with a method **getLocale** that will return the right data
   structure containing the current default locale on the machine
   currently running the applet.

   This means that the applet will run differently on different
   machines. In one country it will speak English, and in another
   it will speak French.

String country=l.getCountry(); This queries the **Locale** object
   and returns a two-character **String** with the country code. You

should note that "Country" could be said to be a property of the `Locale` bean and the `getCountry` has the proper phrasing. There is a small letter 'g', the word 'get', and then the name of the property.

`String language=l.getLanguage();` This produces another two-character country code conforming to the language.

The rest of this method is a fairly lame attempt to produce the right word for the button. You should easily be able to do better than this. In this case, it shows how you might want to assign different words from the same language because different countries speak different versions. Here the folks in the U.S. get "Start" while their ex-sovereigns in the U.K. get "Go". The next line assigns the word "Commence" to all places that speak French. This might include France, Canada, and various islands throughout the world.

Notice that this method also uses English as the default. If someone were to run this applet in Russia, then neither the language nor the country would fit any of the three meager choices in the `if-then` clauses. You should have a default in place for these occurrences.

`jbInit()` This is the main initialization function. The exception throwing mechanism will pass any exceptions generated straight through to the main method `init`, which will catch them and print out the stack.

The main job of this method is to create two versions of `StopLightPanel` and two buttons that will control them.

`light1.addNewLightEventListener(light2);` This line executes the method `addNewLightEventListener`, which is defined in the Event class described later. The main job of this function is to connect up the two classes. It says that if `light1` should generate a new event, then the object, `light2`, should receive notice of the event. The next line connects up the two in reverse so they both know about the events generated by the other.

This is the principal way that Beans communicate. Notice how this setup is constructed. The Beans will receive notice of anyone who wants to hear about the Events they generate and then they'll store them in an internal structure.

Although this chapter doesn't make it obvious, the concept of *persistence* is an important part of Java Beans. This mechanism provides a way for Java Beans to be stored out to disk without losing any of their data.

You should notice that persistence will not affect this construction even though it is not used at all. In the Beans world it is perfectly okay to create two versions of a Bean using the standard `new` system, execute the methods like `addNewLightEventListener`, and then store the Bean away where it will remember these details for life.

This example doesn't use this more enlightened method of software construction. It's just a simple example and you should know its limitations.

`new NewLightEvent (light2, NewLightEvent.Red)` The "events" are really just objects from a class. That's it. In this case, I've created my own event known as `NewLightEvent`. Notice that the phrase `NewLightEvent` should seem familiar. It is also buried inside `addNewLightEventListener`. A major part of the Java Beans movement is the notion of design naming rules. In this case, the event name should end with the word "Event". When the event is used later with listeners, exactly the same format should form the core of the name `addNewLightEventListener`. This makes it possible for an automated program to analyze the different classes and method to determine who reports to whom. If the same name is used throughout, then the automated mechanism can easily determine that it is `addNewLightEventListener` that will be listening for a version of `NewLightEvent`.

The `NewLightEvent.Red` is an integer constant defined inside the event. It is just used to pass information with the Event about what type of event is happening. Here, it means that some light (`light2`) has just turned Red.

`light1.processNewLightEvent` This calls up one of the two stoplights, `light1`, and invokes its `processNewLightEvent` method
to handle the `NewLightEvent` that has just been generated.

The message being carried by this event could be translated
to read "Tell `light1` that `light2` has just turned red." In
this case, this will tell `light1` to turn green. Some critics
reading this code may feel that it would be better to create a
different class of events for communicating between the applet
and the stoplights. Telling one light that the other has turned
red seems like a roundabout way of telling it to turn green.
This is probably confusing the reader more than it should.

This is fair criticism. In an ideal world, that would be a better
way to construct the example. But this is meant to be a short
example and this keeps it simpler. That is its only advantage.
The section on the `NewLightEvent` class should make this easier
to understand.

In a nutshell, this applet creates two stoplights and two buttons.
When one button is pushed, it tells one stoplight that the other has
turned red. That is, it tells it to turn green. Pushing the other
button sends the same message to the other stoplight.

As the text mentions, this method of constructing two new
`StopLightPanel` objects is not the only way to use Java Beans. The
event passing mechanism is designed to make it simple to link up
Beans that already exist. This mechanism can be used extensively
in products like BeanBox for joining together Beans into finished
applications.

Passing Events with `NewLightEvent`

Beans talk to each other through events and this example uses one
class of events known as `NewLightEvent`. Its name was chosen to
conform with the Java Beans design rules, which state that the word
"Event" should be found at the end of the class name for each Event.

There is not much to the code for this class. It's much more a data structure than an object with plenty of methods built into it. In fact, it's not much of a data structure. It really carries only one `int` value with it.

This may seem like plenty of baggage for a simple one-integer message. Why isn't this traveling as a simple parameter to a function call? The answer may go a long way to explaining why Java Beans were created in the first place.

A typical object-oriented collection of methods is linked *statically*. That means that the compiler will take all of the different classes and arrange for the method calls to work. Java has the ability to be linked *dynamically*, and this means that the Beans can be joined together well after they were compiled.

Consider these two lines of code:

```
light1.doNewColor(red);

light1.processNewLightEvent
        (new NewLightEvent (light2, NewLightEvent.Red));
```

Both tell the **light1** object the message "red". The first one, however, is static. The second one tells **light1** to give the message "red" to every object on its list. This is dynamic. A good Bean contains the mechanism for adding objects to and subtracting objects from the list of objects that want to know about events. It's very dynamic.

(The smart reader may want to disagree with how I'm using the word "dynamic". This is fair. Dynamically linked code has traditionally meant that the name of the method is looked up in tables at run time. Statically linked code came with an absolute memory reference that told the program counter to jump to a particular location. Plain Java uses this basic definition of dynamically linked programs. Java Beans goes one step further. The Beans can link and unlink themselves over time. This is a great advantage, but it requires that the event classes be built up.)

Here's the code:

```
package  stop;
import java.util.*;
// This defines a new event, with minimum state.
public class NewLightEvent extends EventObject {
```

```
  static final int Red=0;
  static final int Yellow=1;
  static final int Green=2;
  private int iD=0;
  public int getID() {return id;};
  NewLightEvent(Object source,int i) {
    super(source);
    iD=i;
    }
}
// This defines a listener interface
// for the set of events that
// are generated by NewLightEvent
public interface NewLightEventListener extends EventListener {
  public void doRed(NewLightEvent e);
  public void doYellow(NewLightEvent e);
  public void doGreen(NewLightEvent e);
}
```

This file really defines one class and one interface that may be used in multiple different ways by all of the other classes that use these events.

The two major components are:

NewLightEvent The event itself. This is a descendant of EventObject, the classic event that binds together the AWT.

There are three static constants in the event, Red, Yellow, and Green. These are defined here to enforce consistency. Notice that the names correspond to the three methods defined in the listener.

There is only one element, an integer, in the data structure. This carries the ID of the event. Notice that the constructor calls the constructor from EventObject with the object but doesn't pass along the extra data. This event carries along additional information about the target of the event.

NewLightEventListener This is an interface, which means that it doesn't define any methods themselves. It just defines the structure that they should take. This is a list of the methods that any Bean looking for NewLightEvent should implement if it is going to process the events correctly. This is a standards list.

In this case there are three methods in the list: `doRed`, `doYellow`, and `doGreen`. These are called in response to each of the three different types of events.

A New Bean Called `StopLightPanel`

The goal of this section is to introduce the Bean `StopLightPanel`. This section has taken a roundabout route showing how the Bean is used and how it communicates before actually showing the Bean. This reflects one of the theories about Bean world. The developer should be able to manipulate Beans without looking at the code inside. The developer should be able to use the process of *introspection* to see the methods and events used by a Bean and use them to program the Bean without looking at the source code. This top-down look at a Bean is just a part of that.

Here's the code to the Bean. It is just a stoplight that draws three circles and fills in the right one. The most important part of the code is the section that processes the events. The rest of it should be fairly standard for AWT programmers.

```
package stop;
import java.awt.*;
import java.util.*;
import java.awt.event.*;
import borland.jbcl.layout.*;
import borland.jbcl.control.*;
public class StopLightPanel extends Panel
                implements NewLightEventListener{
  XYLayout xYLayout1 = new XYLayout();
  int lightState=0;
  private Vector listenerList = new Vector();
  public void setLightState(int a){
        lightState=a;
  }
  public int getLightState(){
        return lightState;
  }
  public void cycleLightState(){
        lightState++;
```

```
              if (lightState>2){
                 lightState=0;
              }
    }
    public StopLightPanel() {
       try {
          jbInit();
       }
       catch (Exception e) {
          e.printStackTrace();
       }
    }
     public void paint(Graphics g){
            // Write some stuff on the screen.
       g.setColor(Color.red);
       if (lightState==0){
          g.fillOval(5,5,40,40);
       } else {
          g.drawOval(5,5,40,40);
       }
       g.setColor(Color.yellow);
       if (lightState==1){
          g.fillOval(5,55,40,40);
       } else {
          g.drawOval(5,55,40,40);
       }
       g.setColor(Color.green);
       if (lightState==2){
          g.fillOval(5,105,40,40);
       } else {
          g.drawOval(5,105,40,40);
       }
    }
    public void jbInit() throws Exception{
       xYLayout1.setWidth(60);
       xYLayout1.setHeight(150);
       this.setLayout(xYLayout1);
    }
    // These three functions, doGreen, doYellow and doRed
    // implement the interface,  but they assume that the
    // opposite stoplight has changed to that color.
    public void doRed(NewLightEvent e){
       processNewLightEvent
          (new NewLightEvent (this, NewLightEvent.Green));
       lightState=2; // The other guy reports going Red.
```

```
      repaint();
      //Go Green.
}
public void doYellow(NewLightEvent e){
        // Do nothing for now.
}
public void doGreen(NewLightEvent e){
    lightState=1;
    repaint();
    try{  wait(10000);}
    catch (Exception ee){};
    lightState=0;
    repaint();
    try{wait(10000);}
    catch(Exception ee){};
}
public synchronized void
    addNewLightEventListener(NewLightEventListener l) {
       listenerList.addElement(l);
}
public synchronized void
  removeNewLightEventListener(NewLightEventListener l){
     listenerList.removeElement(l);
}
protected void
  processNewLightEvent(NewLightEvent e) {
  switch (e.getID()) {
    case NewLightEvent.Red:
      for (int i=0; i<listenerList.size(); i++)
        //Send event to all registered listeners
        ((NewLightEventListener)listenerList.
          elementAt(i)).doRed(e);
      break;
    case NewLightEvent.Yellow:
      for (int i=0; i<listenerList.size(); i++)
        ((NewLightEventListener)listenerList.
          elementAt(i)).doYellow(e);
      break;
    case NewLightEvent.Green:
      for (int i=0; i<listenerList.size(); i++)
        ((NewLightEventListener)listenerList.
          elementAt(i)).doGreen(e);
      break;
  }
}
```

}

Here's a line-by-line discussion of the important elements in the example:

import borland.jbcl.layout.*; This section uses a few basic Borland routines for doing the layout. They aren't strictly necessary and probably could be deleted with no consequences. They're here only because Borland's JBuilder was used to create the example.

class StopLightPanel extends Panel The Bean is an extension of the AWT class **Panel**. This isn't too exciting. Many Java programmers may have already extended the AWT by building their own panels. This is one of the points of Java Beans. It's just a layer on top of standard Java and the AWT. It isn't a new thing, it's just a set of rules for building the old thing.

implements NewLightEventListener This class will implement the interface defined by **NewLightEventListener**. This part of the structure simply enforces the rules set out by the event class, **NewLightEvent**.

XYLayout xYLayout1 = new XYLayout(); Part of the Borland layout code. This is a layout manager.

int lightState=0; This is the current state of the light. Red is 0, Yellow is 1, and Green is 2. This is used by the **paint** procedure to determine what to draw.

private Vector listenerList = new Vector(); This is a list of all of the other objects waiting out there to receive notice of any events. It is kept **private** to keep others from monkeying with it. Objects should be added and subtracted only with the right methods **addNewLightEventListener** and **removeNewLightEventListener**.

void setLightState(int a) This method allows you to access the variable (property) directly. Note the structure of the name. The variable, **lightState** began with a lowercase letter and all other words inside the name began with uppercase letters. Now the first lowercase letter is made uppercase and prefaced with the prefix "set". This is the standard name for a method that allows access to a variable. Note that the method should take one parameter of the same type as the variable itself.

`int getLightState()` This returns the value in the property. It also illustrates the standard nomenclature. If you follow this pattern, then the automated routines for analyzing Beans will be able to determine which methods control which properties.

In this example, both `setLightState` and `getLightState` are fairly perfunctory. You should use these simple shells even if you don't want to do anything else here. This isn't just an affectation or a scaffolding for future code that will react to changes in the value of `lightState`. The Beans world focuses upon changing variables through their *access methods*. These are them.

`void cycleLightState()` An extra function added for fun. This is not part of the standard nomenclature although it comes close. That includes only `get` and `set` methods.

`public StopLightPanel()` The constructor calls the method `jbInit` as a way of getting access to the stack in the event of an exception. This is part of the construction used by Borland's JBuilder, although you may want to imitate it yourself.

There is one very important detail in this line that most people won't even notice. There is no parameter for the constructor. At first, you might see this as a consequence of the fact that the class, `StopLightPanel`, is really rather simple. It just doesn't need any information at commencement.

This may be true, but all Beans must come with a constructor that takes no parameters. This is because Beans may be saved to disk and restored later. When this happens, the automatic save and restore mechanism calls the constructor to create the new restored version. There is no way for the automatic restorer to know what parameters to pass in, so the Beans ethic demands that the programmer create at least one constructor that takes no parameter.

There may be other constructors that take a parameter, but these are often only confusing for the user.

void paint(Graphics g) A standard AWT paint routine that paints the right stuff on the screen using the `lightState` as the guide.

void jbInit() Simply uses the standard Borland JBuilder routine to limit the size of the Bean. There is nothing too important here, and it could be left out or modified without destroying the Bean-ness of the example. The layout is something left up to the Bean itself and isn't guided by any of the conventions in the Bean world.

void doRed(NewLightEvent e) This is a standard function that is called when a `NewLightEvent` of type `Red` arrives. There should be one function for each of the different event messages that are passed along. The design conventions suggest that it is best to put a "do" in front as a prefix.

This method is mainly used in this example to respond to a button push. It will be invoked by the applet whenever someone pushes the button. A better nomenclature might call this event a "button push" or a "turn green" command. In this case, I've kept a certain symmetry. A "red" event means that some other light is going to turn red, which means that the light is free to go green. A "green" event means that one light wants to go green so the other better turn red to prevent a conflict and a car crash.

processNewLightEvent ... The function does two things. First, it broadcasts a note to any other listener that it is about to go Green. Then it turns green and repaints itself.

This example shows how a Bean communicates with another Bean. In this case, each stoplight has the other stoplight in its list of other objects asking to be notified of a change. This allows the other light to turn Red and prevent conflict over the color.

The `repaint` command is a standard part of AWT programming.

void `doYellow(NewLightEvent e)` This version does nothing when Yellow comes along. This is just vestigial. It shows what can happen when you use top-down design principles that force you to spell out an event structure before you're sure how the final device will work.

void `doGreen(NewLightEvent e)` This method is invoked whenever the Bean discovers that another Bean is going Green. In this case, the stoplight Bean is listening to only one other stoplight and the other light is announcing that it is about to go green. (It is going green because one of the buttons sent it a red event message.)

`wait(10000);` The light first turns yellow (`lightState=1`), repaints the screen, and then waits a bit before turning red (`lightState=0`).

void `addNewLightEventListener(NewLightEventListener l)` This method follows the standard design rules for naming. It takes the event name (`NewLightEvent`) and adds a suffix ("Listener") and a prefix ("add").

This routine is pretty simple. It just adds the parameter to the `Vector` containing a list of all of the other objects looking for events.

It is synchronized to prevent some weird problems developing if two additions are done simultaneously.

void `removeNewLightEventListener(NewLightEventListener l)` This removes it from the list.

void `processNewLightEvent(NewLightEvent e)` This is the procedure with responsibility for delivering the events to everyone that is listening. It decodes the event and then calls the appropriate method of the object in the list of listeners. This is

why the interface `NewLightEventListener` requires that every
listener implement these functions.

`...listenerList.elementAt(i)).doRed(e);` This method scans
down the list and fires off the right method. If it is a
`NewLightEvent.Red`, then it executes `doRed` for the listener.

Parsing the Events

The most complicated part of this section is decoding the events.
The messages passing between the Beans don't take the most direct
route. The system functions more like a high school gossip network
than the perfect world imagined by our psychiatrists, who are always
encouraging us to be honest and direct. The messages between the
Beans often don't flow directly from one to another.

In this realm, there are three different types of events: `Red`,
`Yellow`, and `Green`. A `StopLightPanel` Bean generates a particular color when it is about to change that color. It is, in effect,
notifying everyone listening that it is about to change.

This example is coded to simulate two stoplights at an intersec-
tion. If one is green, the other should be red and vice versa. When a
Bean wants to go green, it announces it and its partner should turn
red to accommodate it. In the same way, if it wants to go red the
other is free to go green.

In this case, only one of the three possible events is sent between
the two `StopLightPanel` Beans. This is the `NewLightEvent.Green`,
which tells the other one to turn red to prevent a collision. The
`NewLightEvent.Yellow` is never sent in this example and the
`NewLightEvent.Red` is sent only by the applet controlling the
buttons.

A fairly direct way to make this system work would be for each
`StopLightPanel` Bean to have a method like **changeColor** that took
the color as a parameter. This is very simple and straightforward.
You may even choose to use this in some situations. There is nothing
wrong with such an approach and it is not forbidden by the Bean
rules of life.

The main problem is that it doesn't make the event processing mechanism transparent enough for an automatic program to understand. It should be able to determine what events are wanted and generated by a Bean so that others can tune in.

The structure created here makes it possible for other Beans to insert themselves into a listener list *after* the Beans are compiled. This is truly dynamic and it allows a user to take a collection of Beans and string them together to make a final application.

The only thing that is necessary is for a Bean to implement the right interface to get on the listener list.

Conclusion

This section has demonstrated a simple Bean example to show you how to use the Java Beans technology. The most important lesson is that Java Beans are written in Java, *and* they conform to more rigid rules about names and structure.

The next most important lesson is that the Beans should be dynamically linkable. In this case, the linking is done by the applet that creates two copies of the `StopLightPanel` Bean and then links them together. In practice, this linking may be done by the application developer who ships a copy of the three Beans. The main point is that Beans should be able to change the way they interact well after they're compiled.

The third most important lesson is that the event structure is somewhat rigid but is necessary to make this linking possible. If it is done correctly, a meta-tool like BeanBox can be used to link the Beans together.

Each of these lessons is retold in greater detail in the chapters that follow. This is just an introduction, and many of the finer points were missing. There is, for instance, plenty of freedom for a very rich structure for internationalizing the applet. The events can also include vetoable events that let Beans stop others from changing. All of these are spelled out in the future.

To summarize:

- Call the variables by the name "property."

- Give each property a name that begins with a lowercase letter, like "fooBar".

- Create access methods for this property by capitalizing the initial letter and using the prefixes "get" and "set". That is, `getFooBar` and `setFooBar`.

- Events are indicated by creating a class that descends from `EventObject` and ends with the suffix "Event".

- For each event, there should be an interface with a name ending with the suffix "EventListener". This should define the functions that must be implemented to receive that event.

- Each Bean should keep track of the other Beans waiting to hear from it if an Event is generated. They should keep track of this in a flexible queue.

Chapter 3

Fitting In

The Java Beans technology is about making your code fit into a larger scheme so the objects you create can be edited by special tools. This chapter introduces you to design signatures, a concept that is really a set of rules for how to name your methods.

As computer languages evolve over time, their users develop idioms for handling standard events. For instance, in most languages programmers usually use the variable name i to indicate an integer stepping through an array in sequential order. In Pascal, many refuse to use the `goto` command because some computer scientists consider it to be a corrupting influence.

In many cases, the idioms are rolled into the language when a sizable number of people begin to believe in them. When people decided that strong type checking was a good idea, the language Pascal emerged and enjoyed a brief run in (and on) the sun. Today, most of these type checking ideals have been rolled into ANSI-compatable C, which is now practically the same thing as Pascal.

The idioms from object-oriented programming are an even better example. At least several programmers I know said to me, "Oh, so that's OOP. I've been doing that for years." They have evolved the schemes for segmenting their code on their own. Some smart researchers, however, recognized the pattern and worked toward adding the features to the languages. Today, almost every language has object-oriented extensions and Java included them from day one.

The designers of Java Beans faced a problem. On one hand,

they had a set of idioms that they wanted to enforce so that people could build more flexible Java components. On the other hand, they couldn't incorporate their ideas into a new version because they didn't want to break the Java implementations that were on the market. The result is a naming system with the force of law.

In the past, such conventions have been rolled into the language and the compiler would be forced to enforce them. Most of the C++ notions could have been written in C because C is so flexible, but rolling them into the compiler created the opportunity for some deeper optimization of the code.

Since this is not possible, the conventions are enforced by the tools. If you follow the rules, your Beans will fit in nicely and interact correctly. If you don't, they may still compile and run successfully, but you won't be able to use many of the Java Beans tools to manipulate the items.

Design Signatures

The working term for this collection of rules is *design signature*. Some also use the phrase *design patterns*. The terms are fairly descriptive because the collection of rules governs how components are designed. Most of them are applied when a programmer is laying out the structure of the API and deciding which methods need to exist. The word *signature* fits because the rules are more like guidelines that encourage the programmer to leave behind a mark. Just as architects have signature details like the types of columns or composers may have signature patterns of notes, Java Beans forces programmers to have a signature to the structure of their code. This may also be considered a *pattern*.

Many of these conventions will seem obvious to anyone who has programmed in Java before. From the beginning, Sun's Java development team adopted the convention for naming methods with an initial lowercase letter and then capitalizing all of them inside. For instance, the methods `startBombingInFiveMinutes` and `noNewTaxes` obey the rules, but `GCFiVe` doesn't.

There are other basic rules. Classes begin with an initial capital letter. If several words are blurred together, then the interior words are also capitalized. So `WombatLoveEvent` is a valid class name, but `bobTRAINobject` doesn't. Instances of the objects from the classes, on the other hand, use lowercase letters. There are some exceptions. Some of the basic classes that are integral parts of the language, like `int`, use a lowercase letter. Others, like `String`, don't. This distinction is made because `int` is a primitive type that is stored directly to memory, while `String` is implemented as a descendant of `Object`. For the most part, these rules are strong enough because there aren't too many exceptions.

The Abstract Window Toolkit (AWT) also has its own rules, although they were often unspecified. These were obviously the foundation for many of the rules in the Beans design signature. For instance, all of the method calls for changing one of the internal parameters in a class began with the prefix `set`. The methods for finding the information inside began with the prefix `get`. These rules are repeated and extended in the Beans world.

There are four parts to the design signature rules:

Property Access The variables embedded inside a Bean are referred to as *properties*. There are rules for naming the properties and the methods that manipulate them.

Event Sources Events are generated by methods that want to send messages to other Beans in the application. There are rules for naming the sources of the events.

Event Listeners A Bean must make it obvious which events it wants to respond to. These rules guarantee that the container holding all of the Beans will be able to pass the events along successfully.

JavaBeans themselves Of course, the Beans must be named correctly as well. The design signature defines what a Bean must be and what is the minimum it must do.

It is important to realize that these design signatures have close to the force of law. Although it is quite possible to name a Java method `SkiDO042` and have it compile, the same is not true for a Bean. If you name something incorrectly, the Bean features will not work correctly. Actually, there are often tricks you can use to break the rules and still make things work, but you need to do the work. For instance, the `BeanInfo` data structure can be assembled automatically if you name everything according to the signatures, but you can assemble it manually if you have some reason to break the rules.

It is also important to recognize that the naming information is the only information that the Bean technology has. It can't analyze your code and determine that the procedure `readjustFont` acts like `setFont`. Nor can it look inside your `setFont` method and find out that it is really doing something completely different, like downloading a file from an HTTP server. The Bean technology takes you at your word. The names are presumed to be right.

Property Access

A property is just a variable and it may be either a primative type (e.g., `int`, `double`) or an object from a particular class (e.g., `Font`, `Color`, `MyWeirdType`). The properties are changed with an access method, which begins with the prefix `set`.

For instance, a property might be `displayFont`. The initial letter of the property is lowercase because it is not a class name.

Setting Properties

If you built a Bean with this property, then you would set the font with the method `setDisplayFont`. Now, the letter "D" is capitalized because it is an internal word.

The function might look like this:

```
public void setDisplayFont(Font f){
        displayFont = f;
}
```

The function is set to be `public` because it is the default method for accessing this parameter and it must be made available to any other Bean that wants to set this property. The method must also take one parameter, the new property value, and return nothing (`void`).

In many cases, one-line functions like this are a programming conceit. It would be possible to make the property, `displayFont`, public and then simply set it with a simple one-line command:

```
MyObject.displayFont = f;
```

This one-line approach has some advantages. A method call takes time and simply accessing the data directly is much faster. Creating a whole method to do what one line of code does is something that seems overly cautious and almost officious.

But there are other good reasons to do it. The standard explanation given in introductory programming classes is that you may want to add other code later. Creating such an interface now puts the infrastructure in place for modifying the code later. For instance, you may want to compute some data like the height about the font when it is made the display font. This is easy to add into the method `setDisplayFont`.

In the Java Beans world, however, there are even more reasons to create such a property access method. Remember that Beans aren't just packets of code. They are full-fledged objects that carry their data around with them. When you create an instance of `MyObject`, it will create a block of data for holding `displayFont`. This can be manipulated and the changes are persistent. If you set `displayFont` to be 36-point Times, then it will stay 36-point Times.

The advantage of defining property access methods in Java Beans is that any Bean container can let you change the properties directly. An average Bean container, like Sun's BeanBox, can create a Bean object and then let you edit the properties directly. It would be able to examine the object description, find the list of properties, and then match up the properties with the methods that change them. This can be done automatically.

So, even though creating one-line functions like this can be a chore, it has other advantages.

Some access methods take two parameters. In many cases, it makes sense to add an index to the property. For instance, a scrolling menu of choices may have **n** items in the list. A programmer will probably want to change each item individually. The Java Beans format for such a method would look like this:

```
public void setScrollMenu(int i, String s){
        scrollMenu[i]=s;
}
```

Again, this method is `public` and it returns nothing. The index term is the first parameter and the new value for the indexed item is the second parameter.

Getting Property Values

There are also functions for retrieving the property values from inside a class. They begin with the prefix `get`. Here are two examples:

```
public Font getDisplayFont(){
        return displayFont;
}
public String getScrollMenu(int i){
        return scrollMenu[i];
}
```

The basic function takes no parameter and the index function takes only an index. Both are `public` and both return the type of the property.

Again, there are more advantages to creating these one-line functions in Java Beans. A Bean manipulation tool can access the current values of the properties and display them for you to edit.

Boolean Properties

Boolean properties are set just like regular properties with a method that begins with the prefix `set`. Some examples might be `setPrintable` or `setEditable`. But they have a slightly different nomenclature for getting the contents of the variable. They use the prefix `is` instead of the prefix `get`.

Here are some examples:

```
public boolean isPrintable(){
        return Printable;
}

public boolean isEditable(){
        return Editable;
}
```

Both take no parameters and return a boolean value of the property. You may find yourself including other code involved in the test of the property.

Problems and Limitations with this Model

No programming model is perfect, and there are several major problems with this notion of properties and property access functions. In most cases, there are distinct limitations on the range of values stored in a property. This model has no way for a `setProperty` function to signal that the user passed in something outside the acceptable range. The functions must return a `void` and there is no provision for them throwing an exception.

A more robust version of Java Beans might include the ability either to return a value or to throw an exception signaling that the data is out of range. Some programmers throw an `IllegalArgument-Exception` even though it is not part of the design signature. This is a good solution, if you're also going to write the Beans that will have to catch the exception.

Bound Properties

All of the previous examples of property access methods are simple one-line methods. In practice, many programmers end up adding extra code to propagate the effects of the change to other parts. For instance, in many cases changing a font or a point size will require redrawing the screen to bring it up to date.

Simple details can be handled by code within the method, but sometimes you want the changes in the property to affect other classes. You could simply propagate the changes yourself by adding in the proper method calls, but this approach is not really ideal in the Beans world. You want the Beans to be little, individual boxes that get all of their information through regulated channels.

The proper approach is to generate an event to connect them. (The structure of events is described beginning on page 52.) The event can carry the information between the Beans and the event delivery mechanisms can make sure that the information arrives correctly and on time.

Using bound properties is more complex than simply creating property access methods. You must also create additional data structures for plugging into the event delivery system. The major differences are:

1. First, create an instance of the `PropertyChangeSupport` item. This structure will keep track of which other Beans must receive notices of the changes.

2. Add these two methods to your class: `addProperty-ChangeListener` and `removePropertyChangeListener`. These should take a parameter of the type `Property-ChangeListener` and then pass it along to the instance of `PropertyChangeSupport`. These two methods are really just glue logic to keep the information flowing between the different classes.

3. Modify the `setFooBar` property change method to fire off the correct event. It does this in three steps. First, it makes a copy of the old value of `fooBar`. Second, it makes a copy of the new version of `fooBar`. Finally, it calls the method `firePropertyChange` with these two values and the name of the property as a string, ``fooBar". The `PropertyChangeSupport` object will make sure that the data gets to the right place.

4. If the class is also going to receive events, then you must make sure that it implements `PropertyChangeListener`. This means that it offers a method `propertyChange` that does

the right thing with the change. (Building `PropertyChange-Listener` is covered on page 48.)

The code allows a Bean container to group up the Beans and create links between the different properties. It is possible for the Bean programmer to take two Beans, `A` and `B`, and ensure that a message is carried from one to another without rewriting the code. All that needs to be done is for the `addPropertyChangeListener` method of a property in `A` to be called with the name of `B` and `B` will get the message.

Here's an example:

```
import java.beans.*;
public class BoundBackgroundPropertyThing
        extends Canvas implements Serializable {

        Color backgroundProperty;
                // This class really has
                // only one property, the object of our
                // work.

        PropertyChangeSupport pcs= new PropertyChangeSupport(this);
                // This is what is going to
                // handle the dispatch of the messages
                // containing the event information
                // when backgroundProperty changes.
        public BoundBackgroundPropertyThing() {
                backgroundProperty = Color.white;
        }

        public void setBackgroundProperty(Color c) {
                Color oldBackgroundProperty = backgroundProperty;

                backgroundProperty = c;

                pcs.firePropertyChange("backgroundProperty"
                  ,oldBackgroundProperty, c);

                repaint();
        }

        public Color getBackgroundProperty(){
                return backgroundProperty;
        }
```

```
public void
  addPropertyChangeListener(PropertyChangeListener l){
        // These are just glue.
        // They take the information and pass it
        // to the correct PropertyChangeSupport.
        pcs.addPropertyChangeListener(l);
}

public void
  removePropertyChangeListener
    (PropertyChangeListener l){
        pcs.removePropertyChangeListener(l);
}
public void paint(Graphics g){
        // Do the painting.
        g.setColor(backgroundProperty);
        g.drawText("Hello World");
}
}
```

Creating this extra item, the `PropertyChangeSupport`, is a bit of a hassle, but it creates a list of all other items that will want to know about the change in a property. The Bean must be glued in with the seemingly superfluous routines, **addPropertyChangeList- ener** and **removePropertyChangeListener**, which have the simple job of being called to add new items asking to be notified of any changes.

The advantage of this approach is that any Bean carries its own list of other Beans looking for notice of a change in a property. This is bound up within the Bean as the `PropertyChangeSupport` item. There is a standard interface that a Bean manipulation tool can use to add new things to the list of Beans.

Building a PropertyChangeListener

A class must have a particular structure if it is going to be able to receive notification that a property has changed. It must implement the the interface `PropertyChangeListener` which has one function, `propertyChange` in it.

The function **propertyChange** gets one parameter, **Property- ChangeEvent**. This item is just a bundle of the three parameters passed into firePropertyChange. You can access them with the three methods getPropertyName, getOldValue, and getNewValue.

Here's an example of propertyChange:

```
public void propertyChange(PropertyChangeEvent e){
        if (e.getPropertyName=="backgroundProperty") {
                localColor = e.getNewValue();
        }
}
```

This code will simply keep a local copy of the background color used as backgroundProperty. This would allow two Beans to always use the same color and coordinate their appearance.

Two-Way Bound Property (Vetoable)

A bound property is a one-way channel that carries news of a change in the value of a property to another Bean. This information carries both the old and new values of the property. This may be useful in some situations, but it can be quite limiting in others. Imagine, for instance, a nuclear power plant control that takes a value between two end points of x and y. Occasionally, things get out of hand and the values need to be adjusted. One solution is for the control to send out news of the property change and then wait for error messages from other parts of the code. A section of the software that monitored the core temperature of the reactor may decide that the new value could lead to a meltdown.

The class VetoableChangeListener can handle this scenario. It builds a two-way channel between components so that messages can go back and forth. The structure is quite similar to the class PropertyChangeListener described beginning on page 45.

The basic code structure is very similar. You create an instance of VetoableChangeSupport which acts as a clearing-house for the notices of change. Other components are added and subtracted from the list of those to be notified by executing addVetoableChangeListener and removeVetoableChangeListener. Notices of the change are created by executing fireVetoableChange.

The biggest difference is in how the vetoes are carried. They are not shipped as messages carried by the VetoableChangeSupport, but they travel as exceptions carried by the Java exception handling mechanism. More specifically, they travel as a PropertyVetoException

Here's an example:

```
public class VetoableBackgroundPropertyThing
        extends Canvas
        implements VetoChangeListener, Serializable {

    Color backgroundProperty;
            // This class really has
            // only one property, the object of our
            // work.

    VetoableChangeSupport pcs
      = new PropertyChangeSupport(this);
            // This is what is going to handle
            // the dispatch of the messages
            // containing the event information
            // when backgroundProperty changes.
    public VetoableBackgroundPropertyThing() {
            backgroundProperty = Color.white;
    }

    public void setBackgroundProperty(Color c)
        throws PropertyVetoException{
            Color oldBackgroundProperty
              = backgroundProperty;


            pcs.fireVetoableChange("backgroundProperty",
             oldBackgroundProperty, c);

            backgroundProperty = c;

            repaint();
    }

    public Color getBackgroundProperty(){
            return backgroundProperty;
    }

    public void addVetoableChangeListener
```

```
         (VetoableChangeListener l){
              // These are just glue.
              // They take the information and pass it
              // to the correct PropertyChangeSupport.
              pcs.addVetoableChangeListener(l);
    }

    public void
      removeVetoableChangeListener
        (VetoableChangeListener l){
              pcs.removeVetoableChangeListener(l);
    }
    public void paint(Graphics g){
              // Do the painting.
              g.setColor(backgroundProperty);
              g.drawText("Hello World");
    }
}
```

Most of the structure is the same as the implementation of
a PropertyChangeListener. The names are just different. The
major change is that the method setBackgroundProperty now
throws a PropertyVetoException. This exception isn't generated
by setBackgroundProperty, although it could be done in theory.
It originates with the component that gets news of the change in
property values after being told by the VetoableChangeListener.

You may wonder why the Beans developers chose to use an exception instead of another simple event. Although I'm not a developer, I
believe they wanted to avoid the problems of multiple vetoes emerging after multiple components were notified about the problems with
the new value. The Java exception handling and thread management
functions will handle this and they will not need to implement all of
this structure.

The result is that anything that calls setBackgroundProperty
or any method for setting a vetoable property must be ready to catch
the PropertyVetoException. Presumably, the exception can carry
information about what is wrong with the current value passed to it.
This string can be customized by the programmer and adapted to
the task. The programmer should, however, be sure to include the
old and new values of the property. It is entirely possible that several
different attempts at setting the values may become interleaved and

cause trouble. Keeping both values in the message could be enough to keep things straight.

The Veto Generator

The veto generator has its own design signature. The component must:

- Be a class that implements both `VetoableChangeListener` and `Serializable`.

- Have a function, `vetoableChange`, that takes one parameter of the class.

- The method `vetoableChange` must throw exceptions from the class `PropertyVetoException`.

The function, `vetoableChange`, should look something like this:

```
public void vetoableChange(VetoableChangeEvent event)
  throws PropertyVetoException{
      Color c=(Color)event.getNewValue();
      if (c.getBlue()>100) {
              throw new PropertyVetoException
                ("Much too blue. My skin looks bad. Keep blue
                    under 100.");
              }
      }
```

Event Names

Events are a standard part of programming with the Java AWT. You create events, and then the event module ensures that they arrive at a proper event listener. In the Beans world, you need to use the right format for the names of the events so the Beans tools can interpret the events. A tool might allow you to highlight a component and see which types of events it responds to. Then the tool would look for all other components that generate that type of event and offer you the chance to link them up.

The format is fairly straightforward. You create a class that extends `EventListener` and give it a name like `PetesEventListener` or `ExplosionEventListener`.

The class that is going to do the listening, that is, the waiting for an event, must include the function with the prefix **add** and the name of the event class—for instance, `addPetesEventListener` or `addExplosionEventListener`. These functions should take one parameter of the correct class, in these cases either `PetesEventListener` or `ExplosionEventListener`.

There should also be a corresponding method for **remove**-ing the event listener—for instance, `removePetesEventListener` or `removeExplosionEventListener`.

The design signature for these event names also has an option. A listener can throw the exception `TooManyListenersException`. This should be thrown if the event listener can't handle any more Beans asking for updates about a certain event.

Conclusion

The restrictions on naming parts of a Java Bean aren't particularily onerous. Some programmers may chaff at the control, but most should realize that these general rules are necessary whenever anyone works on a large project. Ideally, the realm of Java Beans can become one big, worldwide programming party creating Beans that are flexible enough for everyone to share.

The reality will probably never reach this dream of a harmonic convergence. Programmers are people and Murphy's laws still hold. If you need an object to support some method, it won't. If you find the method you want, it will take parameters in the most inconvenient form. If you do manage to get the data in the right format, you'll usually stumble across one weird case that the programmer never imagined would crash the Bean.

The naming conventions will not repeal any of these problems, but they will make life a bit easier. You'll be able to see inside the code and string it together with meta-programs like BeanBox or JBuilder.

Here are the major lessons:

- Name the variables with names beginning with a lowercase letter.

- Capitalize that letter and add either "get" or "set" as the prefix to let people change that variable.

- You can parameterize the "get" and "set" with an integer. These will be known as "indexed properties." Actually, you can create "get" and "set" routines that will take any arbitrary collection of parameters. The rules of Java still hold. But only those that take one additional `int` will be recognized by meta-programming tools like BeanBox.

- Beans talk with events. Events are just classes that inherit their behavior from the generic class `EventObject`. You should name your events with the suffix "Event".

- Beans must keep track of which other Beans want to hear about the Events they generate.

- Each event "FooEvent" should be accompanied by another interface "FooEventListener" that defines what a class should do when it receives a `FooEvent`. That is, it is a list of methods that should be `public` and available for the Bean generating the event to invoke.

- Beans that support events should have methods with names like `addFooEventListener` and `removeFooEventListener`. A remote Bean that wants to hear whenever another Bean generates such an Event would issue the `add` command.

- Events can also link properties. Some properties can be set up to throw `PropertyChangeEvents` that alert other Beans to the fact that a property changed.

- Some events can also include a feedback mechanism that makes these changes "vetoable".

Chapter 4

Persistence

The term "persistence" and its effects on programming may be the most difficult for a traditional programmer to grasp. The term means that any changes to an object can stick around until the next time the object is used. Although this may not seem too radical by itself, it is the basis for the extreme object-oriented nature of Beans programming.

If changes to a Bean can stick around, then it is possible to create one instance of a Bean and make the changes there. That means it is possible to create a slider bar and then use an access function like `setFont` to change the appearance. This will stick with the slider bar throughout its lifetime.

In practice, the nature of persistence bundles together two effects that are generally implemented in wildly different ways: 1) saving changes in the appearance of the GUI and the action of the components and 2) keeping track of a user's preferences. The first is traditionally done by the programmer who tweaks the C++ code to handle appearances. If the font is switching from `Times` to `Helvetica`, then the programmer probably changes a line in the code from `LoadFont("Times")` to `LoadFont("Helvetica")`. This change is compiled into the final binary code, where it is frozen in time forever.

The second type of change is more fluid. The best code will remember the position of switches, windows, and options by storing these details in a preferences file. The Macintosh has a special directory to hold these files, and they can be found in many places in the PC. These details are kept separate from the binary or object code, which should never change.

In Java Beans, both of these functions blend together because the state of the properties (variables) can stay around. If a Bean implements the interface `Serializable`, then it comes with the ability to save all of its properties to disk so that no data can be lost. The methods in this interface will automatically do all of the work of saving the data to disk for the programmer.

In the past, a wide range of solutions was available to the two different approaches. Most programmers began by freezing everything in code and then slowly made more things flexible by adding functionality to the preferences mechanism. The Beans model moves everything to the other extreme. Suddenly, everything is flexible.

Advantages and Disadvantages

The Bean persistence mechanism has numerous advantages and disadvantages. It is the most radically different part of Bean-land, so these differences should lead many to develop fairly strong opinions about the advantages and disadvantages.

The good news is that the approach frees the programmer from doing any extra work to add flexibility. If there is a variable or property that can be set, it can be made persistent. The programmer doesn't have to do the extra work of manipulating the preferences file.

The Bean mechanism also does all of the saving and restoring of the properties, so the programmer does not need to worry about the types and the bit representation. These details are also consistent across different implementations of Java, so the same Bean will be able to run on Microsoft machines, Macintoshes, and UNIX workstations.

There are also significant disadvantages. If everything is persistent, sometimes details stick around that cause trouble. For instance, a null pointer may cause the program to stop. If the variable is somehow set to `null`, then this could stick around and crash the program

everytime someone tries to restart it. Rebooting the machine won't
make a difference because the image is stored on the disk.

The problem also extends to corporate networks. In the past,
many companies maintained one version of the binary code that was
meant to be a perfect image. People would run this, but their individual preferences would be stored locally on their disk. This solution
is much easier to maintain.

The Beans model, however, bundles all of the preferences into
the code. Everyone could end up with their own version of the Bean
and this would make life rather complicated.

Although a Bean's persistence will often be used for cosmetic
choices, it could end up sowing confusion. Imagine that some variable `defaultTCPPort` is usually set to 80 because the Bean often
communicates with HTTP servers. Someone may install a Bean and
set this variable to 23. This value will persist. Later, when someone
grabs a copy of this Bean, they may run into trouble if they assume
the variable is still set to 80.

A programmer must try to balance these needs and anticipate
when the echoes of past programming will persist through time.

It is important to realize that the process of serialization is con-
trollable. A Bean does not need to save out its state each time it is
shut down. Most of the serialization will occur when a programmer
is knitting together several Beans with a tool like BeanBox. After
that, the components will be frozen together by the serialization process. Then, every user who invokes the system will continue to see
the same look. If the user, however, manages to reserialize the Bean,
then the new data will be saved along with it.

Building in Persistence

Whereas persistence is a difficult chore for humans, it is relatively
simple for Java Beans. There are only two major requirements. The
first is that one of the constructors must take no parameters. It
should create a fully initialized object or Bean with no input.

The second is that the class file must implement the class
`java.io.Serializable` or `java.io.Externalizable`. It is easy to
implement `Serializable|` because you don't have to create your

own versions of any functions. The `Externalizable` interface allows you to add your own methods that do all of the work.

To a large extent, the process of "implementing" the `Serializable` interface is largely ceremonial. There are no procedures that *must* be written. It is more a tag that specifies that you are aware that the data will be saved. Sun's documentation for the interface `java.io.Serializable` says "Classes that do not implement the interface will not have any of their state serialized or deserialized."

Java Beans don't have to implement this interface to be Beans, but if they don't, their data will disappear. This is a good idea only for nonvisible Beans that provide only some interpretation or conversion utility. All components like `Applets` or `Panels` will automatically be serializable because the base class `Component` implements `Serializable`.

You can satisfy the major requirements with a small bit of planning and a few extra words in the code. There are many details, however, that must be thought through. You may not want to simply let the Beans mechanism save every part of a Bean. This could end up introducing strange errors and propagating noise.

The simplest tool for controlling serialization is the `transient` modifier. If you declare a property to be `transient`, then the serializable mechanism will ignore it by default. This is a good technique to use for large data structures like arrays or trees because they will take up plenty of disk space. If the data structures aren't needed in the next round, then you should use the `transient` modifier to keep them out.

Some people mention that you can also use the `static` modifier to keep a property from being serialized. This is true. The Beans model does not try to store variables that are labeled `static` because this data is the same in every copy of the Bean. At best, it would be a waste of disk space and at worst it would be a horrible confusion.

But remember that `static` data is the same for every version of the Bean. If you try to use it to keep data from being written out during the deserialization process, you must be prepared for the fact that each version will share the same variables marked `static`. Use the `transient` modifier if you want to keep it from going to disk.

Avoiding Access Methods

One of the most important things to remember is that the Java Beans persistence mechanism does NOT use the property access methods to get and set the values of the property. Although the Java Beans developers went out of their way to force you to build this functionality into your Beans, they didn't use it at all when they created the Serialization mechanism.

The main reason is probably that not all variables are truly properties. Some variables may be absolutely necessary, but they shouldn't be accessible to anyone. If the access methods with the correct names were available for all properties, then some programmer might try to change them. If you want to keep a property free from tampering, don't create the **set** and **get** methods for access.

Avoiding **set** and **get** methods is also purer. The **Serializable** mechanism will simply try to store a snapshot of the Bean as it stands. It will try to freeze it in time by creating a direct copy of memory. In many cases, access methods can have plenty of side effects and it might be difficult for a programmer to anticipate how the effects would work if all of the properties were set or gotten in a row. The **Serializable** mechanism can't guarantee that the properties are written or read in any particular order.

Using writeObject and readObject

The most powerful mechanism for controlling how objects are serialized is to create your own versions of **writeObject** and **readObject**. These two methods are part of the **Serializable** interface and you can subclass each of them to take control of the process. This allows you do arbitrary things in the process of reading and writing the objects.

The interface is straightforward:

```
private void writeObject(ObjectOutputStream out)
    throws IO Exception;

private void readObject(ObjectInputStream i)
    throws IOException, ClassNotFoundException;
```

Both of these must throw an **IOException** if they can't

complete their job successfully. You may set up code that will catch an `IOException` inside the method, but you must then throw one afterward if you can't correct for the error. The `ClassNotFoundException` is thrown if the reading process doesn't know how to interpret the data coming in. That is, if it is an object of a type without a `.class` file that defines the structure and methods of a class. This might occur if a Bean is deserialized (recovered) on a machine without the right `.class` information.

The interface may be straightforward, but many people may get a bit confused by the name. The stream class also comes with a pair of methods known as `readObject` and `writeObject`. These are *different* and it is important not to get them confused. One pair comes from the classes `ObjectInputStream` and `ObjectOutputStream` and this pair reads and writes data from the disk in object form.

The other pair is created by you, if you want, to control the order in which your own particular class is read or written. In fact, you may call the other pair when you write your own version of `readObject` and `writeObject`.

Understanding `ObjectInput` and `ObjectOutput`

Some low-level Java programmers are already familiar with the interfaces `DataInput` and `DataOutput`. These interfaces specify all of the methods that must be implemented if a class wants to act as either an input or output routine. You might create classes implementing these interfaces if you add a new type of data storage device to a computer system.

The interfaces include methods like `writeChar` or `writeDouble` and essentially make sure that the class can handle all of the basic data types produced in Java. This guarantees that any class implementing the interface will be able to behave correctly when it is called by the central Java system. If a double integer needs to be written, then the interface ensures that there will be a routine available to do the job. `DataInputStream` and `DataOutputStream` are two of the classes implementing this interface.

The Java designers added `ObjectInput` and `ObjectOutput` to do the same job for higher level objects. The interfaces extend

DataInput and DataOutput so they require any implementation to handle all of the basic stuff. The most important methods are readObject and writeObject.

These interfaces are implemented with the classes ObjectInput-Stream and ObjectOutputStream. Both of these classes handle the grunt work of taking apart an object and putting it back together.

The constructors for the two classes are:

```
public ObjectInputStream(InputStream in)
    throws IOException, StreamCorruptedException;
public ObjectOutputStream(OutputStream out);
```

Some Beginning Code

How would you write code that would use these methods? Here's a sample:

```
FileOutputStream fileOut = new FileOutputStream("myFile");
ObjectOutputStream s=new ObjectOutputStream(fileOut);
s.writeObject(new String("Hi!"));
s.writeObject(someRandomObject);
s.writeInt(42);
i=new Integer(42);
s.writeObject(i);
s.flush();
s.close();
```

Notice that the ObjectOutputStream can handle both basic types and objects. This is because ObjectOutput extends DataOutput. In this example, there are two versions of the integer 42 written to disk. The first is written as a basic type and the second is written as an object from the wrapper class of Integer.

This beginning example, however, doesn't explore what would happen with the *other* versions of writeObject and readObject. The variable someRandomObject may come from the class your-FavoriteClass. If yourFavoriteClass was serializable, then it might offer its own version of writeObject or readObject. If you did create these methods, they would be called in turn.

That is, first the method writeObject from the class Object-OutputStream would be called and passed the object someRandom-Object. As that method processed the object and tried to figure out how to write it to disk, it would call the specific versions of `writeObject` that you created yourself.

Writing Your Own `readObject` and `writeObject`

You may want to create your own versions of these methods for a variety of different reasons. Some include:

- Your objects contain data that must be cleaned up. For instance, the words need to be made all uppercase, a list needs to be sorted, or the numbers need to be rounded off.

- Your objects contain data that must be correctly processed. Imagine that your object is a spreadsheet. Some of the items in it are basic variables and some depend upon the values of the others. Recalculating the spreadsheet takes time, so it is done only on command. It makes good sense to recalculate the spreadsheet before saving to make sure that the data stored away is completely consistent.

- You want to limit the amount of data stored away. Some suggest scanning through trees, vectors, and stacks to limit the amount of data in the structure. This saves disk space and keeps everything under control.

- You might want to construct a checksum of the data to preserve integrity. This can be checked later with `validateObject`.

- You may want to encrypt the data or add a digital signature.

Each of these reasons comes from an instinct to keep the data itself clean and neat, not from some desire to write data to the disk in a particular order. In some cases, you may want to write data in a format that could be read by a different computer program. In that case, you should explore implementing the `Externalizable` interface because it is designed to make it easier to write low-level code.

The classes `ObjectInputStream` and `ObjectOutputStream` come with the methods `defaultReadObject` and `defaultWriteObject` to make it easier to do the job. These two methods are somewhat strange. They simply write out the fields that are not static or transient. But this method can be invoked only from a version of `readObject` or `writeObject`, respectively. If they're called at another time, they'll throw a `NotActiveException`.

Here's a simple example:

```
public class SimpleMax implements Serializable {
        int ages[];
        int max;
                // Max should be the largest age.

        private void writeObject(ObjectOutputStream s)
          throws IOException{
                max = ages[0];
                for (int i=1;i<ages.length();i++){
                        if (ages[i]>max) {
                                max=ages[i];
                        }
                }

                s.defaultWriteObject();
        }
    private void readObject(ObjectInputStream s)
            throws IOException,
          ClassNotFoundException{
                s.defaultReadObject();
        }
}
```

This code will make sure that the integer `max` is equal to the largest value in the `ages` array before the data is written out to disk. In this case, the actual writing is done by `defaultWriteObject`.

Writing and Reading Objects Yourself

The last section described how to write your own versions of `writeObject` and `readObject` but showed how to avoid the more complicated parts of writing the objects to the stream. The function `defaultWriteObjects` does the work and the other code simply prepares the way for the data.

This is a fine solution, but there may be times when you want to control what is written to disk and how it is unpacked. The class `ObjectOutputStream` comes with a method `writeObject` that you can execute yourself, and `ObjectInputStream` comes with its own version of `readObject`. You can use these in your versions of `readObject` and `writeObject`. When you do this, remember that there are two different sets of functions with *different* responsibilities but the same name. Sigh.

Here's a basic example that shows how you can control what is actually saved. In this example, the clothing is chosen depending upon the season. In a real example, you may choose to exclude some data because it just takes up too much space and it isn't needed.

```java
class Wardrobe implements Serializable {
  Date today;
  transient LegThings bermudaShorts, swimSuit,
    linenTrousers, woolTrousers;
  // Clothing for the bottom half.
  transient TorsoThings tShirt,poloShirt, woolShirt,
    woolSweater, cottonSweater;
  // Clothing for the top half.
  public Wardrobe(){
    // Null constructor ...
    today=new Date();
    bermudaShorts=null;
    swimSuit=null;
    linenTrousers=null;
    woolTrousers=null;
    tShirt=null;
    poloShirt=null;
    woolShirt=null;
    woolSweater=null;
    cottonSweater=null;
  }
  private void writeObject(ObjectOutputStream s) throws IOException{
    int month=this.today.getMonth();
    s.defaultWriteObject();
    if ((month > 4) && (month <9)){
      // Summer time!! Pack lightly.
      s.writeObject(bermudaShorts);
      s.writeObject(swimSuit);
      s.writeObject(tShirt);
      s.writeObject(poloShirt);
      s.writeObject(cottonSweater);
    } else {
      s.writeObject(linenTrousers);
      s.writeObject(woolTrousers);
```

```
    s.writeObject(woolShirt);
    s.writeObject(woolSweater);
  }
}
public void readObject(ObjectInputStream s)
                        throws IOException{
  s.defaultReadObject();
  // This reads in the date.
  int month = today.getMonth();
  try{
    if ((month > 4) && (month <9)){
      bermudaShorts=(LegThings)s.readObject();
      swimSuit=(LegThings)s.readObject();
      tShirt=(TorsoThings)s.readObject();
      poloShirt=(TorsoThings)s.readObject();
      cottonSweater=(TorsoThings)s.readObject();
    } else {
      linenTrousers=(LegThings)s.readObject();
      woolTrousers=(LegThings)s.readObject();
      woolShirt=(TorsoThings)s.readObject();
      woolSweater=(TorsoThings)s.readObject();
      }
    } catch (ClassNotFoundException c) {
      System.out.println("You need the classes
          LegThings and TorsoThings!");
    }
  }
}
```

This example is certainly contrived, but it illustrates a number of important points about how to handle the reading and writing yourself. These points, in no particular order, are:

- There must be a default constructor that takes *no* parameters. The JavaBeans software will use this constructor to build up the basic shell of the object before handing it off to the readObject routine for filling out.

- The variable today gets filled twice when a Bean is recovered from a disk. First, it gets the current time when the default constructor builds it; then it gets the correct date by executing defaultReadObject.

- The other variables (a.k.a. properties) are *transient*. This means that the `defaultWriteObject` and `defaultReadObject` won't touch them. It's up to you.

- When the objects are read back in, it is up to you to cast them to the correct type. The `readObject` routine will correctly interpret the data and place it in the right locations, but only you know the correct type. (This could be a security hole if you could recover someone else's Beans. This is one reason why the method is `private`. Another is that it shouldn't be subclassed or accessed directly.)

- You can catch the `ClassNotFoundException` when reading things in. If Java can't find the class file that matches the type you're trying to give an incoming object, then it will throw this exception. This could happen if a Bean is recovered on a machine that doesn't have all of the latest class files installed.

  You don't have to catch the exception, however. It can be passed along.

- Don't screw up the order of the items read in. This method is the only place that assigns the data to the name correctly.

This example of a wardrobe with summer and winter clothes was obviously contrived. You may have completely different reasons to leave some parts out of what is stored away from a Bean. The option is yours.

Object Validation

One of the most interesting features of the Beans concept of serialization is the notion of *object validation*. When the Bean is recovered, it is fed to a method known as `validateObject`, which throws an `InvalidObjectException` if something is wrong.

You can write your own version of `validateObject` to do whatever you want. Most people will want to compute some checksum of the data to make sure that it is valid, but you could have it do bizarre things.

Here's an example with the function in use:

```
class ClassRoom implements Serializable, ObjectInputValidation {
   int grades[];
      // The grades.
   int checkSum;
      // Total of all the grades.
   public ClassRoom(){
      grades=new int[100];
         // Assume that there are 100 students.
         // A better solution
         // might use a vector.
      checkSum=0;
      for (int i=0;i<100;i++){
         grades[i]=0;
      }
   }
   public void readObject(ObjectOutputStream s)
     throws IOException {
       s.registerValidation(this,0);
       s.defaultReadObject();
   }
   public void writeObject(ObjectOutputStream s)
      throws IOException{
      checkSum=0;
      for (int i=0;i<grades.length();i++){
         checkSum+=grades[i];
      }
      s.defaultWriteObject();
   }
   public void validateObject() throws InvalidObjectException {
      int tempSum=0;
      for (int i=0;i<grades.length();i++){
         tempSum+=grades[i];
      }
      if (tempSum!=checkSum){
         throw new
         InvalidObjectException("Wrong checksum on grades.");
      }
   }
}
```

The routine **validateObject** is called after the object is built and all of the data is read in. In this case, there is no version of **readObject**, so all of the reading is done by **defaultReadObject**. If no exception is thrown, then the object is put back into use.

In this case, the checksum test could also be implemented in a readObject method. It might be preferable to simply add a boolean flag to the object's properties with the name checkSumValid and set it during the readObject method. This solution would allow the program to continue operating without halting.

In thie readObject routine, the current object is passssed to the method registerValidation. This routine registers the object with a master list. Only these objects are validated when the loading process is complete. The second parameter is a priority number. Zero is the standard value. Larger numbers are called first. You can use this to control the order in which the validateObject routines are invoked when a large tree of objects is restored or deserialized.

If you want the object to invoke validateObject, then it must implement ObjectInputValidation. The routine registerValidation will accept only objects that implement this interface. Note that registerValidation is a routine in the class of ObjectInputStream.

Software Upgrades and Versions of Beans

Software upgrades are a common part of normal life and they often bring a number of different problems. New versions may not read the file structure of old versions. Data in preferences files could become corrupted. Features may appear, disappear, or, even worse, stop working. These are often called *bit rot*.

Software upgrades are a particular problem for Java Beans. The notion of a Bean is a bundle of both code and state that works well as a component with other Beans. Imagine that you have a spreadsheet Bean that is plugged in with other Beans. A new version of the spreadsheet comes out. Ideally, a user will be able to install the newer version without damaging the connectivity with the other Beans or upsetting the data.

Avoiding damaging the connectivity with the other Beans is an important trick. This means that the new version of the Bean must respond to all of the same methods. If there was a method changeFont in the first Bean, then there should be a changeFont method in the new Bean. If there isn't, features that use this will start breaking. This often happens in surprising areas. In this case, any command that lets the user select a font will obviously break. But other computational commands might crash as well if they use a different font to highlight an important result.

The designers of Java Beans tried to anticipate this problem and developed a strategy for creating software upgrades and versions of Beans. This is especially important when Beans "persist" because the new Bean must absorb some of the state of the old Bean.

In fact, Java Beans are surprisingly flexible. They can easily survive adding new methods and even the subtraction of a few important methods. The Beans will break if you start renaming parts of them or change the status of the different properties or variables. But you still have some fairly decent flexibility.

Here are some of the acceptable ways to modify the class functions of a Bean:

Adding New Methods and Properties New data or functions don't get in the way of the old. Java looks up all data and methods by name, so this won't be affected by the existence of new items in the name tables. But this also means that changing the name will destroy continuity.

One of the advantages of using access methods to get at the data in a Bean is that it makes it easier to add new fields to handle future needs. For instance, imagine that the first version of the Bean kept one integer, `fontSize`, to control the appearance of the letters. The programmer wants to add more details about the typeface and a complete `Font` record for the future. This is easy to accomplish if you simply add another completely new variable, say `fontRecord`. Now, a new version of `setFontSize` could be programmed to change both the value of `fontSize` and the details inside `fontRecord`. And, in the same way, `setFontRecord` could change both variables. The old details would work with the new.

What happens if a Bean is stored to disk ("serialized") under the first version of the Bean and restored when the new class files for the new Bean are around? The default constructor (the one that takes no parameters) is used to initialize the object. As the data is read back in ("deserialized"), the fields

are matched up. If data can't be found, the initialized value
is used. The Java compilers for the constructor make sure to
initialize all fields. (This is a major security problem.)

Another way to "add" a property is to convert it from static
to nonstatic or transient to nontransient. That is, take it from
the list of properties that are ignored in the storage process
and move it to the list of properties that are stored.

Changing the `readObject` or `writeObject` Method Surprisingly
enough, you can easily add and delete these methods from a
class file. Both of these methods rely upon default functions to
do the work (`defaultReadObject` and `defaultWriteObject`).
If you add a new version of `readObject` to a class file, it
should call `defaultReadObject` at the beginning. This will
then do everything that Java would do in the background
before the extra function existed.

You can easily add and subtract these methods as long as you
keep track of how the data is written and read from the object
stream. The biggest danger you will face is the optional data
that you may add to the object stream. If you're going to be
saving things to the object stream, then you're going to have to
recover them in exactly the same order. It is your responsibility
to assign the type to the data coming in the object stream, and
it could lead to trouble if you get them wrong.

Changing the Serializable Interface A class is "Serializable" if
it has a constructor that takes no parameters and it implements
the `serializable` interface. This can be accomplished by a few
changes in the basic definition of the class.

You can generally get away with making these changes in either
direction. If you make it serializable, the objects from the class
are suddenly stored away. It's like adding new data. If you
take away the serializability, then the objects from that class
will be treated as if the class file was removed. They'll just be
replaced by null pointers.

This is a surprisingly large amount of flexibility for the programmer. You can add a fair amount of information and change how it is

processed without breaking Beans.

But there are limits. You can't change the names of any variable
without breaking the process of reloading data. Changing the names
of the methods is also bound to break other parts of the interface.
Making variables static or transient has the same effect as changing
their names. You also can't change the types of variables.

Making Classes Externalizable

Most programmers who want to tweak the way that Beans are persistent will want to use the Serializable interface. It is a nice
high-level system for giving the programmers control over the data
that is stored away without requiring them to do too much work.
The default functions handle that for the programmer.

If you want work at a lower level, however, you can utilize
the Externalizable interface. To do this, you must make a class
implement the interface by providing versions of its two methods
writeExternal and readExternal. Here's their definition:

```
public void readExternal(ObjectInput s)
  throws IOException, ClassNotFoundException;
public void writeExternal(ObjectOutput s) throws IOException;
```

Note that Externalizable extends Serializable. So even
though it provides for much more lower level, access to the reading
and writing process, it lives at a higher level in the class heirarchy.
This is often the case in these object-oriented systems. More
features are usually associated with operating at a lower level, and
this means deeper in the class heirarchy.[1]

Notice that these functions work with either an ObjectInput
or an ObjectOutput. These are direct descendants of DataInput
and DataOutput. This means that the class comes with the basic
primitives for writing all of the standard Java types and include
extra functions for dealing with objects. This means you can write
bytes directly to some device or file.

---

[1]Obviously, words like "higher", "lower", and "deeper" start losing their meaning in an abstract world where there is no top or bottom. By "higher" in the
hierarchy, I mean farther from the base case of "object".

The `Serializable` interface, on the other hand, reads and writes from `ObjectOutputStream` and `ObjectInputStream`. These are stream versions that implement the interfaces described by `ObjectOutput` and `ObjectInput`. They're essentially stream versions.

How Beans Are Serialized

When the `writeObject` method is invoked for a Bean, a complicated process begins. All of the properties (variables) are written to disk unless they are either `static` or `transient`. At first glance, this sounds easy. The numbers, strings, or things are written out to disk. The interesting part emerges when the variables hold another Bean or substantial object. The process works recursively, doing a depth-first walk through the tree. Each object is marked in turn, so there is no danger of an endless loop emerging.

Conclusion

"Persistence" is one of the more important concepts in Bean-land and one of the most significant changes between Java Beans and regular programming. This is a much larger departure than Java itself for many programmers. Java, of course, was just another procedural programming language that looked like C, at least on the surface. Persistent Java Beans, however, are another animal. Suddenly the preferences file and the application code are getting mixed together.

Here are the important lessons:

- Persistence is the act of taking a Bean, writing it to a disk file, and then bringing it back to life.

- At the lowest level, it's really just about writing data to a file in the right order and then reading it back in the same order.

- Many of these details are handled by the internal Java routines.

- If you want to override the process, you can do so.

- The easiest way to control whether variables are not saved is to label them `transient`. A more complicated way is to rewrite the routines for saving and restoring Beans to leave out this data.

- The saving and restoration process can be customized on many levels. You can either let it run automatically, do some pre-processing before letting it run automatically, or handle all of the details yourself. This is pretty nice.

Chapter 5

Events

Many Java programmers are already familiar with the concept of an *event*. The Abstract Windowing Toolkit has a class called `Event` and objects from the class are passed around whenever a user touches the mouse or the keyboard. The types of events used to include `MOUSE_DRAG`, `KEY_RELEASE`, and `MOUSE_UP`.[1] The events are passed around the different components in the AWT until one of them takes action based upon the event.

This sort of event-based programming became important to all of the programmers who took up the Macintosh. The core of each Macintosh application had an *event loop* that consisted of two basic steps: 1) check the mouse and keyboard for action and 2) find the right part of the code to take care of this action. This model has been adopted by most modern operating systems. The Windows systems from Microsoft all juggle events and parcel them out to the appropriate application. UNIX systems usually run X-windows, a system that might be the closest in spirit to the Java Beans event model.

Java Beans programmers are going to need to be even more event driven, because the method for communicating between Beans uses the event mechanism. If you want your Bean to tell another Bean to display some message to the user, you'll need to create an event,

---

[1] These are the names from the first version of the AWT. The latest version is now compatible with the new event model described here. These events now come from classes like `MouseEvent` or `KeyEvent`.

pack in the message, and deliver it to the list of Beans that have requested to be notified of new events.

This list of other Beans awaiting notice of events is part of each Bean and is serialized when a new application is created. This is the most important part of the data structure to be serialized and stored for future use, because it controls which Beans talk to each other.

This event-centric gives the programmer the ability to add some object-oriented structure to the messages passed between Beans. The simplest solution is to just create one new event class, `RawDataEvent`, and use it to pass a block of data with internal structure. All Beans could take this event and all could pass it.

This approach simply ignores the possibilities available. Some programmers may want to do this in simple cases (or extremely complex ones), but it is often better to create more rigorous definitions. For instance, a compiler might want to use two different events: `DisplayCompilerWarningEvent` and `DisplayCompilerErrorEvent`. Both of these could be subclasses of the basic `DisplayCompilerMessageEvent`. Different Beans built into the compiler could watch for the most significant errors. Some would trap all of them by watching for `DisplayCompilerMessageEvent`, while others may be more particular and watch only for `DisplayCompilerErrorEvent`.

The Java Beans development team sought to integrate the event mechanism with Java's inherent object-oriented structure. Here are some of the design goals they gave in the Java Beans documentation distributed from JavaSoft:

Provide a Common Framework for Events Java Beans comes with two basic classes: `EventObject` and `EventListener`. (Both are in `java.util`.) When you create your own events, you inherit from `EventObject` and then arrange for a particular class to watch for the events by having it inherit behavior from `EventListener`.

Allow Events to Be Caught and Fired by Scripting Shells Java Beans are fairly independent objects. There is no reason why they can't take information from outside sources like scripts. This allows beginning programmers the chance to string together a number of Beans into a bigger program. Small basic event filtering can be done in the scripting language.

Integrate Events with Application Builders There is no reason why application builders like BeanBox can't control the flow of events between Beans. Many of the application builders for either C++ or Pascal would require the programmer to handle the glue code after the basic skeleton was constructed.

Building events with the correct design allows the Bean application builder to determine which events are generated by which Bean and which can be accepted by another Bean. You can arrange for the action in one Bean to be turned into an event that notifies another Bean. For instance, a button Bean could generate a `startCalculatingEvent` for another computation Bean.

It is important to remember that this approach should be quite abstract. The button Bean would generate the `startCalculatingEvent` for no Bean in particular. The computation Bean would accept the `startCalculatingBean`. Later, when the Beans are knitted together, the BeanBox would add the computation Bean to the list of Beans to be notified of new `startCalculatingEvent` objects being created.

In some cases, the approach may be even more abstract. The button Bean may simply generate a `pushedEvent`, which was interpreted by an event adapter to generate a `startCalculatingEvent` for the calculation Bean. These interpreting tools are known as *event adaptors*.

App Builders Should Know the Important Events The design and structure of the events should make it possible for an application builder to analyze a Bean automatically and determine which events it generates and for which events it listens. This is accomplished with a design signature for the events much like the design signature for properties.

Add a Dynamic Events Clearinghouse The core component of a Beans application must knit together all of the Beans and determine which Beans are listening for which events. All of this is packaged in the event registration mechanism which can take new requests on a dynamic basis. This allows the Beans to modify their relationship over the execution of the program.

Cause No Changes in Java The mechanism passes events by calling up a method on the listener. That is, when a class implements the class `EventListener`, it must produce its own method that will accept events being passed to it. This method is called by the clearinghouse when an event is ready.

This goal was not really satisfied. The first version of the AWT included an event model that was largely abandoned. Now, the latest version of the AWT uses an event model that was standardized with the rest of the Beans world. This isn't really a change in the foundations of Java, but it may be a change to many people using the language who started out with the AWT.

Be High Performance Naturally, every programmer wants "high performance."

Be Familiar Programers migrating code from other component architectures shouldn't be too confused. That is, take into account the design of events in things like AppleScript, CORBA, or SOM.

Basic Events

The events are classes that extend `java.util.EventObject`. By convention, they have the word "Event" as the last five letters of their names like this: `PlanetRevolvesAroundMeEvent`, `AnyTVShow-IsAnEvent`, or `NothingHappenedEvent`.

Here's a basic Event:

```
public class ColorOutOfFashionEvent
        extends java.util.EventObject {
      protected Color badNews;
```

```
      public ColorOutOfFashionEvent(Component source, Color c){
            super(source);
            badNews=c;
      }

      public int getBadNewsBlue(){
            return badNews.getBlue();
      }
      public int getBadNewsRed(){
            return badNews.getRed();
      }

      public int getBadNewsGreen(){
            return badNews.getGreen();
      }

      public Color getBadNews(){
            return badNews;
      }
}
```

This class, `ColorOutOfFashionEvent`, takes two parameters in its construction. The first, `source`, is the component that is generating the event. It might pass a pointer to itself into the constructor with the `this` keyword.

The second is the color itself. It is merely added to the constructor to carry the bad color with the event. This variable is **protected** to prevent unauthorized access. This may not be necessary, because it may be nice occasionally to access the guts of an Event. This is, however, uncool. You should be using accessing methods to set the value.

Event Listeners

For every event that is generated, there must be some method out there to act upon the event. These are classes that implement an interface that end with the word "Listener". The interfaces inherit their behavior from the class `java.util.EventListener`.

Building an event listener requires creating two classes or more correctly, an interface and a class. The interface defines the structure of methods that will actually handle the event. The class provides implementations of these methods that actually do the work. To put it another way, the interface provides an enforceable suggestion and the class does the work.

Here's an example that works with the ColorOutOfFashionEvent from the previous section:

```
interface ColorOutOfFashionListener extends java.util.Listener {
        // Everybody who wants to get ColorOutOfFashionEvent and do
        // something about it, must provide ALL of these methods.

        void callFashionAmbulance(ColorOutOfFashionEvent e);

}
```

When someone builds another component that will handle these ColorOutOfFashionEvents, it may be necessary to add one routine, callFashionAmbulance, that will do the work. It might look like this:

```
public class DesignerErrorHandler
            implements ColorOutOfFashionListener {
  // This might be part of some clothing
  // design software. It could handle all types
  // of errors including bad color ones.
  public void callFashionAmbulance(ColorOutOfFashionEvent e){
     // Code to set up a TCP/IP connection and request an
     // Ambulance sent to the address immediately.
  }
}
```

This shows both halves of the job. The first interface defines what a class must provide in order to receive the ColorOutOfFashionEvent. In this case, there are two handling methods. Both can accept an event of the type.

The design signature or pattern here is simple. The event handlers should accept one parameter of the correct event type. The JavaSoft documentation suggests that there will be cases in which one parameter is not enough. For instance, it suggests that integrating JavaBeans with other component models will require passing multiple arbitrary parameters. The software suggests that developers of application builders should be aware of this possibility and not be doctrinaire in their enforcement of the design signature.

Greater Restrictions

Some suggest that the events and listeners conform to a stronger design pattern. For instance, an event might look like this:

```
public class DogEmergencyEvent extends java.util.EventObject {
        protected int badDogType;

        public final static int BAD_BITE=1;
        public final static int OVER_DROOL=2;
        public final static int MUDDY_PAWS=3;
        public final static int SKUNK_SMELL=4;

        public DogEmergencyEvent(Component source, int type){
                super(source);
                badDogType=type;
        }

        public int getBadDogType(){
                return badDogType;
        }

}
```

This class defines four different types of the dog emergencies that might occur on a trip to the park. There are constants defined for the average user to decode the information in the class.

The constants are `final` and `static` to allow the Java compiler to inline them and understand that they're constant. The variable, `badDogType`, is set to be `protected` to make it inaccessible. This makes it easier for the Java compiler to use the events with synchronized methods. It can assume that no one will try to access the data once the object is constructed.

Here's an interface that might use this structure:

```
public interface DogEmergencyListener extends EventListener {
        public void badBite(DogEmergencyEvent e);

        public void overDrool(DogEmergencyEvent e);

        public void muddyPaws(DogEmergencyEvent e);

        public void skunkSmell(DogEmergencyEvent e);

}
```

This structure is substantially richer than the basic pattern suggested in the Beans documentation provided by JavaSoft. Presumably, if a DogEmergencyEvent was generated with type BAD_BITE, then it would be passed to the method badBite in the DogEmergencyListener.

There are many examples in which the hierarchy allows code to be selective in how it uses events. For instance, the class MouseEvent is a subclass of InputEvent. A component can request access to all events from the class MouseEvent or it could ask for only more general items from InputEvent.

Registering Event Listeners

Each event listener must register itself with the event dispatcher for each other component to get access to events. (The pattern is also described on page 52.) This structure is pretty straightforward, but it has a few basic requirements for how you should structure your code.

The basic restriction is that you must create two methods beginning with the words "add" and "remove" that will add and remove listeners from the list of bits of code that will receive notice of events. The last part of the name should be the interface name of the listener, such as DogEmergencyListener or ColorOutOfFashionListener. You don't need to use this exact format, but if you don't then the automatic routines won't work. You'll need to write your own methods for generating the BeanInfo data structure. (See Chapter 7.)

Here's an illustration:

```
public class VeterinariansHospital {
   private Vector listeners = new Vector();
      // This will hold a list of all listeners who are added.
      // This list will be used to pass out the information.
   public synchronized void addDogEmergencyListener
      (DogEmergencyListener d){
         listeners.addElement(d);
      }
   public synchronized void removeDogEmergencyListener
      (DogEmergencyListener d){
```

```
               listeners.removeElement(d);
      }
  public void notifyDogEmergency(DogEmergencyEvent d){
      Vector v;
      DogEmergencyListener doMe;
      // JavaSoft insists on making a copy of the List
      // of listeners to prevent changes from affecting the
      // list during the notification process.
      // This means that it is threadsafe. Someone may
      // add themselves or remove themselves from the list
      // while this routine is running. This could mean
      // that someone would not get the message.
      synchronized(this) {
         v=listeners.clone();
      }
      for (Enumeration ee=v.elements(); ee.hasMoreElements();){
         doMe= (DogEmergencyListener)ee.getNextElement();
         switch (d.getBadDogType()){
            case
               DogEmergencyEvent.BAD_BITE:
                  doMe.badBite(d);
                  break;
               DogEmergencyEvent.OVER_DROOL:
                  doMe.overDrool(d);
                  break;
               DogEmergencyEvent.MUDDY_PAWS:
                  doMe.muddyPaws(d);
                  break;
               DogEmergencyEvent.SKUNK_SMELL:
                  doMe.skunkSmell(d);
                  break;
         }
      }
   }
}
```

Any component that created an instance of VeterinariansHospital would be able to ask for information about the events by executing addDogEmergencyListener. Remember that the Beans are serializable and they will maintain their data structures through time. A Bean construction applet might create one instance of VeterinariansHospital and then execute addDogEmergencyListener once for each other Bean asking to be notified of DogEmergencyEvents. This information will be stored in the vector, `listeners`, and it will stay with the Bean throughout its lifetime.

In many cases, the method `addDogEmergencyListener` would be executed by the application constructor only when the application was being built. The vector `listeners` could remain unchanged afterward. The method would be executed later only if the application proved to be dynamic and included many Beans entering and exiting the application.

Notice how this structure makes use of the pattern between the names of the various event handling routines and the state of the event. This tag structure is not necessary, but it is a good basic way to handle the event processing.

Unicast versus Multicast Events

The Java Beans developers anticipated the possibility that many Beans may not want to entertain all listeners asking for copies of their events. For this reason, they established the distinction between *unicast* and *multicast* events. This terminology is misleading because the structure of the system is more flexible than this. A Bean can limit its collection of approved listeners to any arbitrary set and it can enforce this rule itself.

The mechanism is straightforward. The addition method (like `addDogEmergencyListener`) can throw the exception `TooManyListenersException` from the `java.util` directory. The method executing `addDogEmergencyListener` must arrange to catch this exception and do the proper thing.

This structure can be very flexible. The class that creates the events can be very discerning about just who it lets into the list of listeners. Here are some of the ways a programmer might choose to implement the addition method:

- Keep the list small. A class may want to broadcast the event to at most n recepients. This lowers complexity and can remove exponential explosion. For instance, imagine that the event listener turns around and fires off its own events in response. If an event is broadcast to two listeners and these, in turn, generate two events, then the system could be flooded very quickly.

- A class could make sure that there was only one listener of a particular type. The listener will implement an interface so there could be many listeners of many different classes. The class could ensure that the data was flowing to only one listener of each class.

- A class could add one type of listener only when another one is present. For instance, it would add a Bean that would play an obnoxious alert noise only if a graphical display was installed. Otherwise, it would assume that the alert noise should not be played because there was no way for a user to understand why it was coming from the speaker.

Event Adapters

The term *event adapter* is often applied to Beans with the job of taking events and interpreting them for another Bean.[2] You may find yourself writing these adapting Beans when you're either working with old code or trying to glue disparate code together. The fact of life is that while object-oriented code is meant to make it easy for people to plug different objects together, they rarely fit together perfectly. Event adapting beans are the translators that keep everything flowing.

For the most part, event adapters are just big if-then-else blocks. If one event comes in, then send out this other event. The structure is not particularly exciting. But there may be cases in which you want to do complex calculations.

---

[2]Calling the adapters "Beans" is a bit of a stretch. They're simple classes with a few decision-making features. They don't generate any interface for the user and they usually sit in the background. It's highly unlikely that a developer will ship an event adapter alone. For all of these reasons, the term "Bean" doesn't seem right. But they do satisfy many of the other very simple definitions.

Vetoable Events

Page 49 of the chapter on design signatures describes the format for vetoable property changes—that is, how to set up a property that announces that it is changing to another Bean. This announcement is carried to a `VetoableChangeListener` that vetos a new value of the property by throwing a `PropertyVetoException`.

Conclusion

Events are the glue that bind Beans. The most important thing is to realize that events are meant to be dynamic, not static. If you were writing one monolithic C or Pascal program, you would probably not use events. If one part of the program wanted to "send a message" to another part of the program, it would probably execute a function call with some parameters carrying the details.

Events, however, are a nice way to bind together different Beans that may not be designed to interact. They replace a compile-time mechanism with a run-time mechanism.

The realm of Java Beans offers a number of events. The simplest ones carry data. More sophisticated ones can allow others to veto the changes and construct a true two-way dialog.

Here are the main lessons from this chapter:

- Beans communicate with events.

- You create an event by subclassing `EventObject`.

- To name an event, choose a name with "Event" at the end—for instance, "MainEvent" or "StopTalkingEvent".

- Each Bean that responds to an event should implement an interface with the name ending in "EventListener". So a class that implements "MainEvent" should implement "MainEventListener".

- You can create arbitrary event structures by subclassing to your heart's content.

- The `BeanInfo` class builds up a list of events that each Bean responds to.

- Chapter 9 contains an example in which two Beans communicate through vetoable events.

Chapter 6

International Beans

For the most part, the world of Java Beans is just a set of rules about how to write programs so they will be reusable. One of the biggest problems for software developers is how to handle different languages and locales. Java Beans includes an entire set of classes known as the *Internationalization API*. They make it simpler to make your program adjust to new locations and display words that the user will understand. The classes won't teach you French or translate it automatically, but they will make it easier for you to do the job yourself.

The major parts of the API are:

A `ResourceBundle` **Class** Resources are an old idea that first emerged in the Apple Macintosh. They've since made their way into the Windows world, and it was only a matter of time before they became part of Java. The idea is to bundle basic parts of the program's appearance in a separate, easy-to-edit location. Instead of hard coding terms like "Click here" inside the code, you can store them in a separate location that can be changed easily afterward.

The Beans Internationalization `ResourceBundle` class allows you to store the different messages in a table. When your program initializes itself, it can check to see where it is running and then choose the right words from the table.

Time Zone Classes The process of telling time is formalized around Greenwich Mean Time. If a user sets up a computer correctly, it will know its time zone. This makes it possible to correct for differences in time brought about by passing messages over the Internet. The important classes are `TimeZone` and `SimpleTimeZone`.

Date Classes Dates are also often different. The folks at Sun have taken this a bit to the extreme because they also offer the ability to use a different calendar. Most of the world uses a Gregorian one, but they've provided the functionality to change. These classes include the base class `DateFormat` and its main instantiation `SimpleDateFormat`. You can create your own by creating a `DateFormatData` class. The base class for the calendars is `Calendar` and its main instantiation is the class `GregorianCalendar`.

Formatting Classes Many countries format numbers and dates differently. Some countries, for instance, use a comma every three digits. Others use the comma as a decimal point. These classes will format numbers for you correctly. These include the `NumberFormat` base class and versions of `NumberFormatData`.

String Formatting Many languages say things in different ways. For instance, an English version may say something like "The word 'tongue' is not in the database." But a French version may write " 'La Langue', ce n'existe pas". The English version put the word in the middle of the string, while the French version put it at the beginning.

In cases like this, it is not enough to have different versions of the text available in a table. They must also be formatted differently. Beans offers a way for you to provide different subclasses that will do the right formatting based on the location running the program. These let you inject procedures for formatting the code, not just templates.

Font Management Fonts are important because many parts of the globe don't use straight ASCII text. Many include different diacritical marks and others use completely different alphabets. Java is built upon the 16-bit standard Unicode that includes many of the more common letters. The `String` classes use these, not ASCII. Most of the work was already done before Java Beans came along.

Still, many will use the `FontMetrics` class to measure the size of text in order to make items fit correctly.

Splitting Words Most text editors will scan over text and allow you to select either a letter, a word, a line, or a sentence. Many languages, however, have different definitions of what these mean. There are a number of different classes that take apart the text. These include the `CharacterIterator` interface and its main implementation `StringCharacterInterator` and the `TextBoundary` class.

The most important part of creating an international Bean is probably using the `ResourceBundle` class to include a number of different ways of formatting dialog boxes and interface tools to say something intelligible to the user.

The next most important part is using the correct library calls for things like formatting numbers and dates. If you use the libraries, they will automatically adapt to the country where the program is being run. If you use your own code, then you'll either have to do the work yourself or the functionality will be hampered. The most important thing is to know that the classes exist.

Only the more ambitious will find themselves using the other tools to create their own ways for splitting text or formatting things. The option is available to you, but most won't need to use it.

`Locale` and How to Use It

Java distinguishes between country and language because the same language is often spoken with a different dialect in different parts of the world. The basic notion of a region is embodied in the base class, `Locale`. Here's a list of the different ones:

Code	Language	Country	Language Constant	Country Constant
da_DK	Danish	Denmark		
de_AT	German	Austria		
de_CH	German	Switzerland		
de_DE	German	Germany		GERMANY
el_GR	Greek	Greece		
en_CA	English	Canada	ENGLISH	CANADA
en_GB	English	Great Britain	ENGLISH	UK
en_IE	English	Ireland	ENGLISH	
en_US	English	United States	ENGLISH	US
es_ES	Spanish	Spain		
fi_FI	Finnish	Finland		
fr_BE	French	Belgium	FRENCH	
fr_CA	French	(Quebec)	FRENCH	CANADA FRENCH
fr_CH	French	Switzerland	FRENCH	
fr_FR	French	France	FRENCH	FRANCE
it_CH	Italian	Switzerland	ITALIAN	
it_IT	Italian	Italy	ITALIAN	ITALY
ja_JP	Japanese	Japan	JAPANESE	JAPAN
ko_KR	Korean	Korea	KOREAN	KOREA
nl_BE	Dutch	Belgium		
nl_NL	Dutch	Netherlands		
no_NO	Norwegian (Nynorsk)	Norway		
no_NO_B	Norwegian (Bokmal)	Norway		
pt_PT	Portuguese	Portugal		
sv_SE	Swedish	Sweden		
tr_TR	Turkish	Turkey		
zh_CN	Chinese	China	SIMPLIFIED_CHINESE	PRC
zh_TW	Chinese	Taiwan	TRADITIONAL_CHINESE	TAIWAN

The first part of the code in the first column of the table is the language code, which is derived from the list of two lowercase letter codes defined by ISO-639. The second part is the ISO country code defined by IOS-3166. The two are joined into a member of the `Locale` class by the constructor that takes the two as `String` parameters. The codes in the first column of the table are generated by the `toString` function from actual objects from the `Locale` class.

The fourth and fifth columns offer constants for common configurations. These are `final` objects defined by the `Locale` class. To use them, you'll need to include the class (`java.util.Locale`) or preface the constant with the right path information. For instance, England is `java.util.Locale.UK`.

Another version of the constructor takes three parameters. The first two are the language and country codes. The third is a *variant* that could include information about the platform (Macintosh, Sun, Windows, Netscape, etc.). The code from the table for the Bokmal version of Norway is another way that the variant can be used.

This list is clearly far from complete and it is as interesting for what it includes and what it doesn't. For instance, political lines are respected by concluding that there just might be a difference between English in the United States and Canada. But regional lines are generally ignored. The different languages in Switzerland are included, but the different dialects from China are not. But the implementation is sensitive to the distinction between China and Taiwan. There is also another constant, `CHINA`. In the long run, this list will need to grow substantially.

Using the class `Locale` is generally not very hard. Many classes for formatting data have been extended to take the `Locale` as a parameter. If it is not available, then a parameter-free version returns an answer, usually assuming the United States and English. If there is enough information in the system at run time, then it might even use the right local language.

For instance, you can execute `NumberFormat.getPercentInstance()` and this will return a `NumberFormat` object with information about how to format a percentage in the default `Locale`. You can also feed this method a `Locale` parameter by executing `NumberFormat.getPercentInstance(java.util.Locale.FRENCH)` and it should produce the right formatting information for using French.

Keys and Key Properties

The Abstract Windowing Toolkit (AWT) is intended to run on many different machines manufactured by many different people. The world, of course, is a complicated place, and many people have had different ideas about the best way to implement things like the function keys (F1–F12) and keys like insert. This information is kept in a mapping that the AWT uses at initialization time.

You can fiddle with these lists and change the mappings. They are stored as `Properties`, which is a class that is a descendant of the `Hashtable` class. It matches `String` to `String`. In this case, the strings include ones like `AWT.f4`, which stands for the AWT version of F4.

Creating Your Own ResourceBundle

The class ResourceBundle is used to create the mappings between
a Locale and a String. You'll probably want to create these classes
to help change the values of different strings in your user interface.

The base class, javainResourceBundle, can be extended by over-
riding two methods, getKeys and handleGetObject. The first function, getKeys, must return an Enumeration object with a set of
elements containing all of keys that are available to search for in the
class. The keys in this case aren't keys from a keyboard but strings
that are used in the mapping.

The second function, handleGetObject, must do the work of
responding to the keys. That is, given a key as a String, it must
return the right string that matches it. One key may be "Greeting",
and the English version should return "Hello" while the Spanish
version should respond with "Hola".

Using the ResourceBundle class hierarchy is a bit complicated
because the name of the Locale is coded in the name of the
class. That is, you might create a class MySalutationResources which is a subclass of ResourceBundle. Then you would
create MySalutationResources_es for Spanish resources and
MySalutationResources_fr for French ones. Both of these would
be subclasses of MySalutationResources.

If you wanted to create a special class for French Canadian salu-
tations, you would build MySalutationResources_fr_CA, which is
a subclass of MySalutationResources_fr. All of these examples
return Strings. They can return any object. The keys must be
Strings.

This seems to be a bit problematic, at first, because the standard
solution would be to create a huge database that took in the Locale
and the key before returning the answer. But this solution utilizes
the object-oriented class hierarchy to save work. It is possible for
you to define a huge collection of answers for English and define only
a few specialized solutions for the individual countries.

A good way to explain it is by an extended example:

```
abstract class MySalutationResources
  extends ResourceBundle {
```

```
    public Object handleGetObject(String k) {
        if (k.equals("greeting")) {return "Hello"; }
        else if (k.equals("leaving")) {return "Good Bye";}
        else if (k.equals("transition")){return "By the way";}
        else {return null;}
    }
    public Enumeration getKeys(){
        Vector answer = new Vector(3);
        answer.addElement("greeting");
        answer.addElement("leaving");
        answer.addElement("transition");
        return answer;
    }}
abstract class MySalutationResources_en_CA
    extends MySalutationResource {
    public Object handleGetObject(String k) {
        if (k.equals("greeting")) {return "Hello, eh"; }
        else if (k.equals("leaving")) {return "Good Bye, eh";}
        else if (k.equals("transition")){return "Eh";}
        else {return null;}
    }}
abstract class MySalutationResources_fr
    extends MySalutationResource {
    public Object handleGetObject(String k) {
        if (k.equals("greeting")) {return "Bon jour"; }
        else if (k.equals("leaving")) {return "Au revoir";}
        else if (k.equals("transition")){return "Mais";}
        else {return null;}
    }}
abstract class MySalutationResources_fr_CA
    extends MySalutationResource_fr {
    public Object handleGetObject(String k) {
        if (k.equals("greeting")) {return "Bon jour, eh"; }
        else {return null;}
    }
}
abstract class MySalutationResources_es
    extends MySalutationResource {
    public Object handleGetObject(String k) {
        if (k.equals("greeting")) {return "Hola"; }
        else if (k.equals("leaving")) {return "Hasta la vista";}
        else {return null;}
    }
}
```

This set of code produces five classes. The function **getKeys** is found only in the top class, `MySalutationResources`. If it is called in any class, then it will return the `Vector` containing a list of the different keys. In this case, there are only three of them.

The class hierarchy helps minimize your work. Notice that the methods `handleGetObject` will return `null` if they can't find the right answer. This will be passed up the chain of the hierarchy checking for the right answer.

For instance, if the `Locale` is `fr_CA`, then it will return "`Bon Jour, eh`" to the request for the key "`greeting`" but a plain "`Au Revoir`" to the key "`leaving`". The method `handleGetObject` in `MySalutationResources_fr_CA` returned a `null`, so the job was passed up the chain to `MySalutationResources_fr`.

Notice that the base class for all of these is `MySalutationResources`, which just happens to answer in English. It is the respondent of last resort. It is also called when a class for an individual locale is not defined. Passing the key "`greeting`" with the Norwegian locale will still respond with "`Hello`".

Using the Resources

When the resource classes are built, they must be accessed. There are several major routines that you may choose to use:

```
public final Object getObject(String key)
    throws MissingResourceException;
public final String getString(String key)
    throws MissingResourceException;
public final String[] getStringArray(String key)
        throws MissingResourceException;
```

The first routine, `getObject`, is the main way to access the resource bundle, although all of the routines from the previous example return a `String` in response to a request for a key. Most people will probably use the system in this way, but it was made more abstract. You can store any type of `Object` bound to a key. The key, however, must be a `String`.

The other two functions, `getString` and `getStringArray`, are designed to save you the trouble of having to typecast the object returning from a search. This is just a bit of syntactic sugar.

Of course, these routines are worthless if you don't know to which class they belong. They are part of the class `ResourceBundle`, which means they must be executed upon a `ResourceBundle` object. But how do you know the right `ResourceBundle`? Execute a static method call:

```
Locale l=Locale.getDefault();
ResourceBundle mR=ResourceBundle.getBundle("MySalutationResources",l);
```

In this code, the `Locale` is set by calling the static method `getDefault`. It will pull up the default that should be set somewhere by the applet. You can also create your own `Locale` with the constructor methods or use one of the static constants built into Java 1.1.

The method `getBundle` will search for the right files containing the resource specified by the name in the first parameter. The second parameter, the locale, is optional. The `getBundle` command is smart and it will try to find the best match for the current `Locale` by working its way up the hierarchy.

Imagine, for instance, that you had executed

```
Locale l=Locale("fr","CA","Mon");
```

This set `l` to be French Canadian with the "Mon" variant for Montreal. The classes defined beginning on page 94 don't define one for this variant, but they do offer one for the more encompassing `fr_CA`. The `getBundle` command will load this bundle into memory as `mR`.

The command works its way up the hierarchy. If no matching locale is found, then it uses the default. Choose the default well.

ListResourceBundle for Simpler Resources

For many occasions, the whole process of creating methods that answer the requests for keys is just too much work. People want a simple one-to-one mapping and they want it now. There are two classes that make this easier to implement. The first, `ListResourceBundle`, maintains the resource bundle as a two-dimensional array. The other, `PropertyResourceBundle`, uses a file set up in a specific format.

The `getBundle` command can load property files as well. See page 99.

Creating a `ListResourceBundle` is quite simple. Instead of defining all of the methods in the class hierarchy, you simply create two-dimensional arrays. You must create one function, **getContents**, that returns this two-dimensional array. The class of `ListResourceBundle` will do the job of sorting through this array and returning the right value to a call of **handleGetObject**.

This next example is just a version of the set of **ResourceBundle**s described on page 94. It should do exactly the same thing, but it uses arrays to do the job. Obviously, the code from page 94 could have been more complicated. It could have used some additional state to control just which resource was returned. It might have, for instance, used a random number to choose between greetings, or it could have used a static variable to rotate them.

```
abstract class MySalutationResources
   extends ListResourceBundle {
       public Object[][] getContents(){
             return c;
       }

       static final Object[][] c = {
             {"greeting","Hello"},
             {"leaving","Good Bye"},
             {"transition","By the way"}}
}
abstract class MySalutationResources_en_CA
   extends MySalutationResource {

       public Object[][] getContents(){
                 return c;
             }
       static final Object[][] c = {
             {"greeting","Hello, eh"},
             {"leaving","Good Bye, eh"},
             {"transition","Eh"}}
}
abstract class MySalutationResources_fr
   extends MySalutationResource {

       public Object[][] getContents(){
                 return c;
             }
       static final Object[][] c = {
```

```
                {"greeting","Bon jour"},
                {"leaving","Au revoir"},
                {"transition","Mais"}}
}
abstract class MySalutationResources_fr_CA
   extends MySalutationResource_fr {

        public Object[][] getContents(){
                    return c;
            }
        static final Object[][] c = {
                {"greeting","Bon jour, eh"}}
}
abstract class MySalutationResources_es
   extends MySalutationResource {

        public Object[][] getContents(){
                    return c;
            }
        static final Object[][] c = {
                {"greeting","Hola"},
                {"leaving","Hasta la vista"}}
}
```

In this case, all of the versions of `MySalutationResource` are subclasses of `ListResourceBundle`, which means that their version of `handleGetObject` will work with a version of `getContents` to do the work. Notice that each version of resource bundle comes with its own version of `getContents`. This guarantees that the right version of `c` will be returned.

PropertyResourceBundle and File-Based Resources

From time to time you may want to store your resources in a file that can be edited. The class files used in the previous two examples, beginning on pages 94 and 98, both use class files. Any changes must be made by using a Java compiler to rebuild the class files. The concept of a `PropertyResourceBundle` removes this restriction by storing the resource information in a simple text file.

The distinction between a class file and a Property file is lost on the method `getResourceBundle`, which has the responsibility of finding the right resource bundle to match a locale. If you give it the right locale, it will load up the correct one based on the name.

The names for Property files containing resources for internationalization are straightforward. The first part is the name of the class,
such as "MySalutationResources", the second is the two-letter code
of the language, and the third is the two-letter country code. If you
want to add more levels, you're welcome to add a fourth part for the
region.

For example, the file "MySalutationResources_fr_CA" would hold
the resources for the class `MySalutationResources` for the French
language localized in Canada.

The `PropertyResourceBundles` take on a simple text format.
Here's what the file "MySalutationResources_en_CA" would look
like:

```
greeting=Hello, eh
leaving=Good Bye, eh
transition=Eh
```

This file holds a set of `String`s. In practice, you can also record
any collection of serializable objects, but the method for editing arbitrary objects from a text editor is really too complicated. A better
solution is to create them programmatically.

Here are the steps:

1. Create an instance of the class `Properties`. This is a descendant of `Hashtables`.

2. Add the different objects to the class with the method `put`.
   That is, execute `p.put(key,object)`, where p is the instance
   of `Properties`, `key` is the `String`, and `object` is an arbitrary
   `object`.

3. Create a file by opening an `FileOutputStream`.

4. Save the data by executing `p.save(file,"Default`
   `Properties")`.

Remember that the `ResourceBundle` class can handle objects in
only three forms: `Object`, `String`, and `StringArray`. You will need
to cast the object to the right type if it isn't one of these three.

Format for Different Languages

C programmers will feel at home with the Java Beans system for formatting sentences, numbers, and choices in different languages. The Beans designers felt that there needed to be an easily accessible collection of functions for doing more than just customizing the objects returned by the `ResourceBundle`. That is, different languages don't always do things in a way that can be easily handled by the database mapping of `ResourceBundle`.

MessageFormat and Sentence Reformatting

One class includes a method for reformatting sentences to take advantage of the differences between languages.

For instance, consider the four sentences: "Yes, red is the color of my true love's hair.", "Yes, brown is the color of my true love's eyes.", "Her hair is brown.", and "Her hair is red.".

These four sentences come from these two patterns: "Yes, %0 is the color of my true love's %1" and "Her %1 is %0". The two tokens, "%0" and "%1", are wild cards that are replaced with "red" and "hair" in one case and "brown" and "eyes" in the second.

This system could be used either to randomize the output or to correct for differences between languages. German, for instance, often places the verb at the end of the sentence, whereas other languages usually place it near the beginning.

The simplest solution is to pass an array of objects to the pattern and let the static version of the `format` method do the work. You can also create your own patterns with fairly complicated approaches to inserting text. This basic version, however, just uses the `toString` method to convert the object into a string.

```
Object[] args = new Object[2];
args[0]= "red";
args[1] = "hair";
String pat="Yes, %0 is the color of my true love's %1.";
String a1=MessageFormat.format(pat,args);
pat = "Her %1 is %0.";
String a2=MessageFormat.format(pat,args);
```

This simple call will apply the `toString` method to the objects in the `args` array (not too hard) and then insert them into the pattern.

More complicated constructions can be used with `Date` objects and some of the other formatting functions. Here's a different example:

```
Object[] args={
        new Date(System.currentTimeMillis());
        "string"}
String pat="On {0,date} at the time of {0,time},
        a {1} is still a {1}.";
String a1=MessageFormat.format(pat,args);
```

This will produce a string such as `On Aug 1, 1997 at 9:45 AM, a string is still a string`.

The `MessageFormat` class also comes with the ability to go backward and parse a message given the format. This method, `parse`, is really pretty powerful, but it isn't perfect. You should plan on using it only with strings that are generated from the pattern. It also can't deal with ambiguous references.

If you're going to use the `parse` method, you'll need to create an object from the `MessageFormat` class that is customized for the particular pattern. The `MessageFormat` constructor takes one argument, a `String` holding the pattern, and builds a special table. You may also want to use this constructor if you're going to be using the same pattern over and over again because the static version shown above will run the constructor each time it is called with `format`.

Here's an example:

```
String pat="Yes, %0 is the color of my true love's %1.";
MessageFormat mf=new MessageFormat(pat);
Object[] a=pat.parse("Yes, purple is the color
        of my true love's hair.");
```

NumberFormat and Numbers

Numbers are also formatted into different structures depending on the locale. The class `NumberFormat` will convert either a `double` or a `long` into a string by inserting the correct commas and periods.

Here's a simple example:

```
NumberFormat n=NumberFormat.getInstance(loc);
String a = n.format(dub);
```

In this example, the `loc` holds the locale that you want. You can set this either with one of the constants (`Locale.CANADA`) or by constructing a `Locale` object with the right codes. The variable `dub` is a double precision number. If you call `getInstance` without a parameter, it will return the default.

The effects of the `format` method are controlled by a number of access methods. For instance, `setMaximumFractionDigits` and `setMinimumFractionDigits` will do exactly that. They'll control how many digits of a real number will be kept after the decimal point. The functions `setMaximumIntegerDigits` and `setMinimum-IntegerDigits` will control how many of the digits are kept to the left of the decimal point. All four of these methods take a single `int` as their parameter.

There is also a feature that allows currency to be formatted differently. In the United States, for instance, there are only two decimal points of precision in breaking apart the dollar, and the amount is preceded by a dollar sign ($). Other countries place the symbol after the amount. The method `getCurrencyInstance` works like `getInstance` but it returns the special version of `NumberFormat` designed to handle the currency for the `Locale`. There are also other versions, such as `getNumberInstance`, which finds the right format for a regular number, and `getPercentInstance`, which will format a percentage.

You can also find the list of `Locales` that have special `NumberFormat`s installed. The static method `getAvailableLocales` will return an array of `Locales` for you to scan.

The class `NumberFormat` is an abstract class, which means that you need to use one of the descendants if you want to create your own version of the `NumberFormat`. In this case, the most applicable would be the `DecimalFormat`.

If you want to create your own `DecimalFormat`, there are two ways to approach the job. The first is to grab a copy of an existing format and customize it using the access methods. This is quite easy and to be recommended. The second is to specify all of the patterns in the right grammar and pass it to the `DecimalFormat` constructor. This is beyond the scope of the book (i.e., the author).

Here are some of the access methods that you can use to change a `DecimalFormat` object. Most take `String`s as parameters.

`setPositivePrefix` This is the string that is put in front of positive numbers. It is usually blank for regular numbers, but it may be set to be a symbol in currencies. In the United States, for instance, it is "$".

`setPositiveSuffix` If a positive number comes with a suffix, then this should be nonblank. This may happen in Japan, for instance, where the symbol for yen often comes after the amount.

`setNegativePrefix` This is usually a negative sign, but it may be set to be an open parenthesis, which is used in some accounting to show a negative number. Obviously, any currency symbols should also be included.

`setNegativeSuffix` This should be a close parenthesis in the cases in which parentheses are used to show negative numbers.

`setMultiplier` This takes an `int` and it is usually set to be 100. This is the amount by which the number is multiplied to be turned into a percentage.

`setGroupingSize` The number of digits between a grouping separator. In the United States, the grouping separator is a comma and the grouping size is 3.

Each of these functions also comes with a companion beginning with the word `get`. You can use the `get` versions to get the `String` serving as the prefix or suffix. Use it if you're curious.

The symbols for a `DecimalFormat` are stored in a data structure known as the `DecimalFormatSymbol`. You can get and set the version used by a particular `DecimalFormat` with the methods `getDecimalFormatSymbol` and `setDecimalFormatSymbol`.

The fields in the `DecimalFormatSymbol` can be set with these methods. As before, there are companion versions with the `get` prefix if you're curious. All take `char` values unless otherwise specified.

setDecimalSeparator The symbol that comes between the integer part of a number and the fraction. In the United States it is a period.

setGroupingSeparator The symbol that separates groups of the integer part of the number. In the United States, this symbol is a comma. You can control the number of digits between the groups by executing `setGroupingSize` and applying it to the `DecimalFormat` object.

setInfinity The `String` returned when the number gets out of control. Often the string `Inf`.

setMinusSign This is `char`, which comes before negative numbers. Make sure that this does not conflict with the negative prefix set in the `DecimalFormat` that uses this version of `DecimalFormatSymbol`.

setNaN The not-a-number symbol that is returned on division by zero.

setPatternSeparator If you're going to be adding your own patterns to the `DecimalFormat` object, then you'll need to separate them. This is usually a semicolon. (This book doesn't really explain how to use the pattern feature.)

setDigit If you're going to be adding your own patterns to the `DecimalFormat` object, then you'll want to use a character to specify a generic digit. This is that character.

setPercentage The character that symbolizes a percentage sign. In the United States, it is %.

setPerMill A character used for a mille percent sign.

setZeroDigit The character used as a zero. If a number begins with a zero, then this is not printed in most numbers. But serial numbers or other databases often print it.

ChoiceFormat for Linguistic Accuracy

Sun added the class of `ChoiceFormat` to deal with the problem of plurals—that is, finding a way to create a dialog box that will say that there are either "no errors", "one error", or "142 errors". The "s" should be accurate in a well-developed piece of software.

The class `ChoiceFormat` descends from `NumberFormat` and offers the world a `format` method that can be called by a `MessageFormat` routine. The current implementation of the class doesn't offer much Internationalization. The JavaBeans documentation suggests that you don't create a `ChoiceFormat` by calling `getInstance`.

In a sense, the `ChoiceFormat` is just a long case statement that converts a range of `double` values into a `String`.

Here's an example:

```
double[] limits=0.001,0.01,0.1,1.0,10.0,100.0,1000.0,1000000.0;
String[] names={"fractions of a cent",
      "pennies",
      "dimes",
      "dollars",
      "tens of dollars",
      "hundreds of dollars",
      "thousands of dollars",
      "millions of dollars"};

ChoiceFormat f=new ChoiceFormat(limits,names);
System.out.println("I have "+f.format(1231.32)+" to my name.");
System.out.println("Bob has "+f.format(42424211.32)+" to his name.");
System.out.println("Mary has "+f.format(0.1)+" to her name.");
```

The `ChoiceFormat` code will search down the array `limits` looking for the first entry that the value is greater than or equal to. In this example, I will have "thousands of dollars" to my name, Bob will have "millions of dollars", and Mary will have "dimes".

The `ChoiceFormat` class also comes with the `parse` functions that are part of a descendant of `Format`. You can use them to undo the choice made by the class.

The fact that `ChoiceFormat` is a subclass of `NumberFormat` means that you can plug the class into a `MessageFormat` to format complete sentences. Here's an example:

```
Format[] ff={f,NumberFormat.getCurrencyInstance()}
```

```
MessageFormat mf=new MessageFormat("{1} is {0}");
mf.setFormats(ff);
Object[] oo=1422.0,1422.0;
System.out.println(mf.format(oo));
Object[] oo=4124224.0,4124224.0;
System.out.println(mf.format(oo));
```

This code will produce the sentences "$1422.00 is thousands of dollars" and "$4124224.00 is millions of dollars."

Date Classes for Formatting Time

There are two major classes in the world of time in Beanland. The first, `GregorianCalendar`, implements the abstract class `Calendar`. This is part of the Java scheme for turning one particular day into some representation of years, months, days. It includes functions like `before` that will compare two days in Gregorian time. It is entirely conceivable that some others will implement their own base classes to represent their own calendars.

The second major class is `DateFormat`, which works with the other `Format` descendants to turn dates into a `String`. You would use this to specify a standard way to represent a Date in text format—for instance, "Sun Dec 5, 1997 12:14:44".

Conclusion

The International API is not a crucial part of making Beans interact, but it is an important part of making your Beans usable throughout the world. It provides multiple different ways for you to customize your Bean so that it will display different languages and formats in different parts of the world.

Some programmers may not imagine their Beans living beyond their personal machines. Others may want to achieve worldwide dominance in the software world. If you want the second, then the system can be quite useful.

It is important to realize that the system is not limited to languages. It is possible to add a third level of the hierarchy beyond the locale and the country. Normally, this might be used to adapt to an even tighter location. Like, California, for sure. But you can also use this third level to create your own customization. For instance, you might customize the name of a ball team or some other detail about a customer's installation. It doesn't need to be geographic at all.

Here are the important details from this chapter:

- A program can identify the location of the machine on which it is running by the `getLocale` method built into applets and other components.

- The `Locale` data structure consists of three strings. The first is the language, the second is the country, and the third is an optional modifier that you can use as you wish.

- The simplest way to use the `Locale` data structure is to load it and interpret it yourself using some `if-then` statements. This may create a lot of code, but it is the simplest approach.

- Java 1.1 also provides several other mechanisms that make it easier. You can store your strings in resource files and ask Java to load the most appropriate resource files.

- You can also create `ResourceBundle` classes that have methods that execute. The most appropriate one will be loaded based upon the `Locale`.

- There are also internationalized methods for formatting dates, times, and numbers.

Chapter 7

Using BeanInfo

Most of the information in this book is really just a set of rules for how to write code in certain situations. The chapter on events (Chapter 5) shows how to write code that will pass information between beans in the right events format. The design rules (Chapter 3) show how to give your methods the right names so that everything fits together correctly.

The `BeanInfo` object is what pulls all of these rules together. This object carries all of the information about the inside of the Bean and it allows a construction program to help you string together Beans. These Beans-aware applications are the end goal of the entire system.

The process of revealing the interface and API of a Bean is called both *introspection* and *core reflection*. Both terms are meant to express how an object that was once fairly opaque reveal information about its data structures and how to manipulate them.

The `BeanInfo` object is meant to express much more about the Bean. It should tell which properties are there, how they can be changed, which events are important, and more. The interface is completely customizable, so you can write your own routines that tell only part of the story if you wish. Or you could include customized versions that provide more elaborate information.

The end goal is a Bean that can be manipulated automatically by a programming tool. This will make it easier for programmers to include your Bean in an application and link up all of the parts correctly.

BeanInfo Interface

The BeanInfo class is really an interface. This means that it doesn't come with any of its own methods. It's just a completely abstract class. If you want to implement any of the features, you should create your own version of the methods. Otherwise, the automatic reflection will do the job.

The core method is getBeanInfo. This will return the BeanInfo object for a particular Bean. This version of BeanInfo may be one constructed specifically for the Bean, or it could just be pointers to the automatic routines that will use the design specifications to analyze a Bean. Most users probably won't want to take the time to implement their own version of BeanInfo because the code can be larger than the Bean itself. But the option is available.

The method itself comes from the class java.beans.Introspector. This will invoke the right method for the particular Bean in question. In most cases, this will be the automatic code that will use the naming rules to figure out the properties, events, and the methods for changing them.

If you do create your own version of BeanInfo for your own class MyClass, then you should name it MyClassBeanInfo. Just append the words "BeanInfo" to the end of the class name. These linguistic conventions may be a bit of a kludge and the result may be long names, but they do the job.

Here are the main routines from the BeanInfo interface. Most programmers will call these when they're looking for a particular routine inside a Bean. You may also want to implement them in your own version of BeanInfo.

getBeanDescriptor This returns a descendant of FeatureDescriptor known as BeanDescriptor. This includes most of the information about the Bean, such as its name and a few flags about it.

getEventSetDescriptors This comes back with an array of EventSetDescriptor objects. This array contains information about all of the Events that a Bean will respond to. It includes

information about how to add listener methods to link together the objects that generate an event with those that lis-
ten for them. `EventSetDescriptor` is also a descendant of
`FeatureDescriptor`.

`getDefaultEventIndex` This returns an `int` that is the index
of the event that is usually used with this Bean. Use
`getEventSetDescriptors` to decode the information.

`getPropertyDescriptors` This returns an array of `PropertyDes-`
`criptor` that contain basic information about all of the properties. These include information about the property's type
and how to read and write to it. You can also check to see
if the property is bound and which `VetoableChange` events it
will generate if you change it. `PropertyDescriptor` is also
a descendant of `FeatureDescriptor`, so it contains the basic
information about the names of the basic properties.

`getDefaultPropertyIndex` This produces an `int` that represents
the property that will "mostly commonly be initially chosen for
update by the humans who are customizing the Bean." That's
what the Sun documentation says. I can't imagine any reason
why this method would be essential, but you may discover it.
It is generally used to make it easier for people to use tools like
the BeanBox to glue properties together. This is the first one
in the selection list.

`getMethodDescriptors` This also comes back with another array
that contains all of the information about the different methods
available to the public that wants to access the Bean. This is
really just some information about the name and the list of the
parameters. `MethodDescriptor` and `ParameterDescriptor`
are also descendants of `FeatureDescriptor`.

`getAdditionalBeanInfo` Let's say, for some reason, that one
`BeanInfo` is not enough. This will allow you to return multiple
versions of `BeanInfo`. This could be useful if you wanted to
return a list of other Beans that are connected.

`getIcon` Each Bean may come with a number of different icons that
can display it on the screen. There are two types of sizes (16×16
and 32×32 pixels) and two color schemes (color and black
& white). The function must return an image. The method
takes a parameter that is an integer defined by four constants
(`ICON_COLOR_16x16`, `ICON_COLOR_32x32`, `ICON_MONO_16x16`, or
`ICON_MONO_32x32`).

Each of these functions should return a `null` if it has no particular
information. This is a clue to run the automatic processing to analyze
the lists of methods and properties.

Notice that there are only `get` routines here. You can't `set` any
of these functions. This is a bit of a security precaution. There is no
real reason why someone other than the Bean's creator will want to
fool around with the information about the guts of a Bean. So there
is no reason to include these functions.

Of course, you could implement access functions if you wanted to
do so. The correct way to do it is to subclass the `SimpleBeanInfo`
class and provide your own methods for answering the queries. Then
you can make the `get` routines say whatever you want.

FeatureDescriptor

All of the basic descriptors returned by the `BeanInfo` routines are
descendants of the `FeatureDescriptor` class. Here are the basic
properties and methods from this basic foundation:

`getName` The name of the Bean, method, property, or event. This is
often quite important because it is used when you're scanning
through the list looking for one in particular. The name is the
only tool for making sure you have the correct item.

`setName]` This allows you to set the name. It takes a `String` as a
parameter.

`getDisplayName` You may want to have a true name for the Bean,
method, property, or event and then have one that is revealed
to the world. If you want to have a different one, then you can

set the `displayName` property and this is what will be displayed
to the user.

setDisplayName Used for modifying the display name.

isExpert A `boolean` method that defines an "expert" flag. The
"expert" methods, properties, and events may be kept away
from some people if you desire.

setExpert For changing the `expert` property.

isHidden The `hidden` property allows certain events, methods, and
properties to be kept out of sight of the average user manipulating a Bean. This is different from the `public/private` control
of the methods. The `hidden` information is still available to
the public, it's just that a well-intentioned Bean manipulation
software won't display it. Of course, hackers (or serious programmers) may write their own code and completely ignore the
`hidden` boolean.

setHidden For controlling the `hidden` property. Takes a `boolean`.

getShortDescription Returns a `String` that is supposed to be a
description of the event, Bean, property, or method. If none is
specified, the function will return the `displayName`.

setShortDescription This lets you change `shortDescription`. It
takes a `String`. The Java Beans documentation suggests that
this should be shorter than 40 characters to fit nicely on the
screen.

setValue This method takes two parameters: a `String`, which acts
like an attribute name, and an `Object`, which is matched to it.
You can use this to add your own information and properties
about an object to the descriptor.

getValue Takes a `String` and finds the right `Object` to match it.
You'll need to type cast it.

attributeNames This returns the `Enumeration` of all of the at-
tributes that are stored in the database built by `setValue`.

This is only a list of Strings. There is no information about the types.

All of these basic methods are available to each of the subclasses like BeanDescriptor, MethodDescriptor, PropertyDescriptor, or EventSetDescriptor.

This means that it is fairly easy to write your own code to iterate through the list printing out information. Here's some simple code:

```
public void
  outputFeatureDescriptor(FeatureDescriptor[] fD){
    for (int i=0;i<fD.length;i++){
      System.out.println(fD[i].getName()+":"+
        fD[i].getDisplayName()+":"+
        fD[i].getShortDescription());
    }
  }
public void showBeanStuff(Class b){
    try{
      BeanInfo bI=Introspector.getBeanInfo(b);
    } catch (IntrospectionException e) {
      System.out.println("Can't find the Bean's information.");
      exit();
    }
    outputFeatureDescriptor(bI.getMethodDescriptors());
    outputFeatureDescriptor(bI.getPropertyDescriptors());
    outputFeatureDescriptor(bI.getEventSetDescriptors());
}
```

MethodDescriptor Stuff

The MethodDescriptor is a descendant of FeatureDescriptor. There are two extra functions that you can use that apply only to methods:

getMethod This returns an object from the class Method. This isn't a pointer to the method itself, but you can use it to run the method if you choose. The function invoke will run the method and take a list of parameters. This approach will allow LISP programmers to use their tricks with Java, because it makes it fairly easy to implement eval-like behavior.

getParameterDescriptors This routine returns an array of
ParameterDescriptors. These include information about all
of the different parameters and what they do. See page 119
for information on these data structures.

There are also two constructors for the class. One takes a simple
Method object while the other takes a Method object and an array of
ParameterDescriptor objects.

Your best solution is to let the built-in Java Beans methods construct this object for you.

PropertyDescriptor Stuff

This data structure holds descriptions of the properties (i.e., variables) bound into each object. The information in this data structure is used to link together the object automatically because it gives
information on how to change the different properties. The introspection is fairly powerful because the automatic constructor can
determine whether a property is "bound", that is, if it will send off
a PropertyChange event when something happens.

The main constructor for a PropertyDescriptor object takes a
String with the property name and a Class object with the class.
It will analyze the contents of the class and fill out the data struc-
ture. This isn't too brilliant because it relies upon the names of the
methods to do the matching. So if you pass in the variable name
"Peter", it will search for the methods getPeter and setPeter.

There are also more complicated versions of the constructor that
will let you pass in methods for identifying the correct get and
set methods. So you could arrange for arbitrarily complex naming schemes to work here. But I don't recommend this.

When the data structure is completed, you can access the data
with these methods:

getPropertyType This returns a Class object that defines the class
of the data held inside the property. It usually tries to figure
this type out by looking at the response of the get method for
accessing the property.

Note that the function may return a `null` if the property is indexed and there is no nonindex access method. In this case, the place to look for the type is in the class of objects `IndexedPropertyDescriptor`. (See page 116).

getReadMethod This returns an object from the `Method` class. Obviously, this is the method with the `get` prefix. `getGetMethod` must have sounded weird.

getWriteMethod This returns an object from the `Method` class. This is generally the method with the `set` prefix.

getPropertyEditorClass Just a `Class` object, but the one that can let you mess around with the contents of the property. The Class is invoked by applications like the BeanBox to let people modify the property. These classes can be quite elaborate if you want. For instance, you could provide an entire color wheel for selecting a color. If it is `null`, then one will probably be found automatically.

setPropertyEditorClass In the unlikely event that you need to mess around with this yourself, you can use this `set` routine.

isBound Bound properties send `PropertyChange` events when they're changed. This function returns a `boolean` describing whether this happens or not.

setBound Pass this method a `boolean` to tell it what you want to say about a property.

isConstrained If a property is controlled by another object with veto power over a change, then this method will return a `true` value. Otherwise, it will return false.

setConstrained If you need to change the value of the constraint on this property, pass a `boolean` to this method.

IndexedPropertyDescriptor Stuff

An `IndexedPropertyDescriptor` object is a subclass of the more basic `PropertyDescriptor`. It is used because some properties are "indexed", that is, they are an array and need to be accessed with an array index. All of the standard methods from `PropertyDescriptor` are at work here, but some won't work as before. `getWriteMethod`, for instance, may fail and return a `null` if there are only indexed write methods.

The basic constructor will take a `String` and a `Class` and use the naming convention rules for identifying the elements. If these are too constraining for you, there are also constructors that allow you to pass in your own methods for doing the job.

Here are the new methods:

`getIndexedReadMethod` Returns a `Method` object for the method responsible for giving you access to the data inside the property.

`getIndexedWriteMethod` Returns a `Method` object corresponding to the method used for changing the property.

`getIndexedPropertyType` The `Class` representing the type of data stored away.

`EventSetDescriptor` **Stuff**

The `EventSetDescriptor` is a subclass of `FeatureDescriptor` and its job is to carry information about the nature of the events to someone or something interested in the action going on inside a Bean.

Most of the way to program events is covered in Chapter 5 and this includes determining which methods are used to add and subtract events from the listener list.

`getListenerType` When an event comes in, this is the `Class` of the interface that is destined to handle the event.

`getListenerMethods` This is an array of `Method` objects that list the methods to be invoked with this event arrives. They are part of the Interface class.

`getListenerMethodDescriptors` Like `getListenerMethods`, but the response is an array of `MethodDescriptor` objects. This might save you some time.

`getAddListenerMethod` This is the method for the `Class` that will add a new Listener waiting for an event.

`getRemoveListenerMethod` The `Method` of the event listener.

`setUnicast` A unicast event is delivered to only one listener. This method takes a `boolean`.

`isUnicast` A `boolean` function for testing a particular event.

`setInDefaultEventSet` This takes one `boolean` parameter that determines whether an event is in the "default" event set. That is, it is generated by default.

`isInDefaultEventSet` Returns a `boolean` based upon whether it is in the "default" or not.

There is a wide variety of constructors for an `EventSetDescriptor`. Most include various ways of adding your own methods for filtering through the methods and identifying the crucial events.

The easiest constructor to use takes four parameters: the source class that generates the events, the name of the event set, the class of the listeners out there, and the target methods for the listener. When you use this simple constructor, it assumes that you've followed the basic rules for naming everything. That is, if the basic name is "OpenWindow", then the event should be named `OpenWindowEvent`, and the interface should be the class `OpenWindowListener`. The methods `addOpenWindowListener` and `removeOpenWindowListener` should do the work of removing them. Here's the format:

```
public EventSetDescriptor(Class sourceClass,
                          String eventSetName,
                          Class listenerType,
                          String listenerMethodName)
```

The other constructors are described in the API information.

`ParameterDescriptor` Stuff

When a method takes a parameter, the Java Beans introspection process will assemble a record about the parameter. The `Method-Descriptor` comes with one property filled with a list of the parameters. This is the data structure that holds the information. It is, like the rest of the descriptors, a descendant of `FeatureDescriptor`. But, unlike the other descendants of `FeatureDescriptor`, there is no specialized information added. All of the methods and variables are found in the `FeatureDescriptor` class. This may change in the future, but the most important information about the name is there.

`BeanDescriptor` Stuff

The `BeanDescriptor` is a descendant of the `FeatureDescriptor` that carries some basic information information about the Bean itself. That is, it carries information about the various names and descriptions.

There are only two access methods in the definition of the class. One, `getBeanClass`, returns the class object describing the class and the second, `getBeanCustomizer`, returns the class that will help customize a Bean. Both can only be set by the constructor for the `BeanDescriptor`. In fact, both are passed in as parameters.

The Introspection Class

The first part of this chapter described the class `BeanInfo`, which was just the top of a big data structure containing information about all of the methods, their parameters, the events, and the properties of a Bean. This data structure doesn't emerge out of nowhere. It must be built by some process.

Most people will be perfectly happy with the automatic constructors for `BeanInfo` that are built into the 1.1 version of Java. This can be accomplished by calling **getBeanInfo** with the name of the Bean. Here's a line of code that will cause the entire data structure to be constructed:

```
BeanInfo bI=Introspector.getBeanInfo(myBeanClass);
```

The `Introspector` class contains a static method, `getBeanInfo`, that will try to construct the right `BeanInfo` version. Again, the naming rules are a big constraint here. If your Bean is named "Bob", then it will look for the class `BobBeanInfo` and try to run its constructor.

If you haven't constructed your own descendant of `BeanInfo` for your particular class, then Java will build one for you. It will use its own "low-level reflection to study the methods of the class and apply standard design patterns to identify property accessors, event sources, or public methods."

This means that if you use the right design patterns, then Java will be able to construct most of the `BeanInfo` for you. This is probably the best goal for everyone using Beans. There is the functionality for you to hide methods or make things behave differently in special situations, but I recommend using those features only in extreme cases. It will make everything simpler.

Here are the basic methods in the `Introspector` class:

getBeanInfo This exists in two versions. The first takes only one `Class` object pointing to the base class of the Bean. The second takes an additional `Class`. This is known as the "stop point." Both versions will scan the class and assemble information about the various parameters, methods, properties, and events. If a "stop point" is mentioned, it will not go deeper in the hierarchy than that class. This makes it possible to concentrate only upon the methods, classes, and whatnot that were added in the lowest layer.

decapitalize This converts a `String` into a Java variable name. This is necessary because the program will automatically look for properties using this rule. The standard solution is to change the first character from uppercase to lowercase if it is necessary. But there is an exception. If there is more than one uppercase letter at the beginning of the `String`, then it leaves it untouched. "MyProperty" becomes "myProperty" and "URL" stays "URL".

getBeanInfoSearchPath This is where the `Introspector` class will search for your own personalized `BeanInfo`. That is where it will look for `BobBeanInfo`.

`setBeanInfoSearchPath` This is how you can specify it to the class if you want.

Building Your Own BeanInfo

The method `getBeanInfo` is a great tool for analyzing random Beans and assembling all of their methods, fields, and events into a coherent data structure. The only problem with the basic `getBeanInfo` is that it will use the basic naming conventions to assemble the data. That means if you have a variable with the name `fredsAge` and you happen to write a method `howOldIsFred`, the basic introspection will skip right over that method. It will be looking for the method `setFredsAge`.

This situation can occur in a number of different ways. Some people may be retrofitting old code that was written before the Java Beans rules for naming were created. Others may feel that it is a free country and they want to name their methods whatever they want. (Pity the fool who tries to update their code.) Still others may want to deliberately obfuscate their code to make it harder for people to analyze it. Still others may just have their own reasons for naming something different.

Of course, there are other reasons as well. You might want to block the user from knowing about certain properties, methods, or events. This technique is not perfect because a smart programmer could use some of the lower level core reflection methods described later in the chapter. But it will still obscure these details in many of the basic tools on the market that use the `BeanInfo` data structure to give access to a Bean.

In any case, Sun was smart enough to provide a way for authors of a class to create their own private `BeanInfo`. All you need to do is create another class with name created by taking your class name and adding the suffix `BeanInfo`; that is, `Foo` begets `FooBeanInfo`, `MyPanel` begets `MyPanelBeanInfo`.

This class must implement the abstract interface `java.beans.-BeanInfo`. There are two ways to do this. The macho way is to assemble the entire data structure on your own. A simpler approach is to make your class extend `SimpleBeanInfo`, a basic `BeanInfo` constructor that follows all of the naming rules. You can simply override the methods that you want to change.

The basic parts to the `BeanInfo` interface are described on page 110. You must implement all of them: `getBeanDescriptor`, `getEventSetDescriptors`, `getMethodDescriptors`, and `getPropertyDescriptors`. There are also ones like `getDefaultPropertyIndex`. This is the item in the array returned by the `getPropertyDescriptors` that the author believes may be the most likely property for someone to access. (An editor offering access will point to this property first.)

One of the more interesting, or perhaps bizarre, elements of this API is what happens if any of these routines return a `null`. In this case, the `getBeanInfo` doesn't pass along the `null`—it goes and uses automatic introspection to assemble the data. This isn't a particularily great approach if you actually want to pass along no information, but it makes it easier to spin up your own version of `BeanInfo`. The correct way to pass along no information is to return an empty array with length zero. (`return new X[0]`).

An Example: BIEx

Here's an example constructed as a simple applet with a few properties: `first`, `second`, and `third`. A new class, `BIExBeanInfo`, was created in order to hide the existence of `third` from the average Bean user. That is, this subclass of `BeanInfo` creates its own list of `PropertyDescriptor` objects and conveniently leaves out the property `third`.

The applet needs to have its own version of `BIExBeanInfo` because the access methods for `first`, `second`, and `third` have nonstandard names. If you want to get the contents of `first`, you execute `WhoIsOnFirst`, not the standard name `getFirst`. The class `BIExBeanInfo` is responsible for putting this information together correctly.

There are a few other notable details in this version of the basic applet BIEx. The method `fattenPath` will add the current package to the path searched for the correct version of `BeanInfo`. If you end up storing the right `BeanInfo`, then you should use a function like this to change the path searched for the right class. In this case, the function isn't used because the class `BIExBeanInfo` is stored right next to the class file for `BIEx`.

```java
package BIEx;
import java.awt.*;
import java.awt.event.*;
import java.applet.*;
import java.beans.*;
import java.lang.reflect.*;
public class BIEx extends Applet {
BeanInfo bi=null;
String[] where;
String first;
int second;
double third;
public String whoIsOnFirst(){
  return first;
}
public void whoShouldBeOnFirst(String s){
  first= s;
}
public int whatIsOnSecond(){
  return second;
}
public void whatShouldBeOnSecond(int i){
   second=i;
}
public double DoYouKnowWhosOnThird(){
  return third;
}
public void LetMeTellYouWhosOnThird(double d){
  third=d;
}
  public void outputMD(MethodDescriptor[] fD){
    for (int i=0;i<fD.length;i++){
      System.out.println(fD[i].getName());
      }
    }
  public void outputPD(PropertyDescriptor[] fD){
    for (int i=0;i<fD.length;i++){
```

```
        System.out.println(fD[i].getName());
        System.out.println
          ("Read It:"+fD[i].getReadMethod());
        System.out.println
          ("Write It:"+fD[i].getWriteMethod());
      }
    }
  public void fattenPath(){
      String[] a1,a2;
      a1=Introspector.getBeanInfoSearchPath();
      a2=new String[a1.length+1];
      for (int i=0;i<a1.length;i++){
        a2[i]=a1[i];
      }
      a2[a1.length]="BIEx";
      Introspector.setBeanInfoSearchPath(a2);
  }
  //Initialize the applet
  public void init() {
    try{
        bi=Introspector.getBeanInfo(this.getClass());
    } catch (IntrospectionException ie){
    }
    outputPD(bi.getPropertyDescriptors());
    System.out.println("----------------------");
    System.out.println("----------------------");
    outputMD(bi.getMethodDescriptors());
 }
  //Get Applet information
  public String getAppletInfo() {
    return "Applet Information";
  }
}
```

The BIExBeanInfo for Introspection

When the applet described above executes the line Introspector.getBeanInfo(this.getClass()), the static method in Introspector attempts to find the right BeanInfo to return. In this case, the class BIExBeanInfo is found in the search path. This has the right name and it implements the interface BeanInfo so it assumes that it has found the right class.

When the applet executes a line like bi.getPropertyDescriptors(), the Introspector first goes to the class **BIExBeanInfo** and executes the method. In this case, the class provides a version of **getPropertyDescriptors**, so it fires it up and asks for its answer.

The method **getPropertyDescriptors** is surprisingly straightforward. It merely creates an array and fills it by executing the constructor. In this case, the constructor has the names to be passed out hard coded.

Note that the method **getMethodDescriptors** returns a **null**. This **null** does not get passed along to the user. The **Introspector** class interprets this as some sort of error and then tries to use automatic scanning to construct the result. The same could happen if **getPropertyDescriptors** happens to hit some sort of **IntrospectionException** that is caught by the block of code that returns a **null**.

Notice that this example extends **SimpleBeanInfo**, a basic **BeanInfo** class provided by the folks at Sun. This can save you the trouble of implementing all of the **BeanInfo** interface. In this case, there isn't much difference between this version of **getMethodDescriptors** and the version being overridden in **SimpleBeanInfo**. Both return **null** and let the automatic scanning in **Introspector** do the work.

```
package BIEx;
import java.beans.*;
public class BIExBeanInfo extends SimpleBeanInfo{
    public MethodDescriptor[] getMethodDescriptors() {
      return null;
    }
  public PropertyDescriptor[] getPropertyDescriptors() {
    Class beanClass=null;
    try {
       beanClass=Class.forName("BIEx.BIEx");
    } catch (ClassNotFoundException c){
    }
    try{
      PropertyDescriptor[] pd  =
          new PropertyDescriptor[2];
      pd[0] = new PropertyDescriptor
          ("first",
          beanClass,
          "whoIsOnFirst",
```

```
            "whoShouldBeOnFirst" );
        pd[1] = new PropertyDescriptor
            ("second",
            beanClass,
            "whatIsOnSecond",
            "whatShouldBeOnSecond" );
        return pd;
    }
    catch(IntrospectionException ie){
    }
    return null; }
}
```

The Results

Here are the results of executing the applet BIEx.BIEx. Notice that the first call to outputPD produces only the properties reported by BIExBeanInfo. The second call to outputMD, however, produces all of the public methods held by the applet. Notice also that some of properties being hidden by BIExBeanInfo are visible here. This is because the automatic scanner developed this list. For instance, LetMeTellYouWhosOnThird is buried in the list. It is hard to keep information away from other Bean users who are executing the Bean unless you make methods private.

```
first
Read It:public java.lang.String BIEx.BIEx.whoIsOnFirst()
Write It:public void BIEx.BIEx.whoShouldBeOnFirst(java.lang.String)
second
Read It:public int BIEx.BIEx.whatIsOnSecond()
Write It:public void BIEx.BIEx.whatShouldBeOnSecond(int)
-----------------------
-----------------------
isActive
whoShouldBeOnFirst
addMouseMotionListener
handleEvent
getCodeBase
addFocusListener
action
setLocale
print
createImage
removeNotify
```

```
showStatus
getComponents
move
getForeground
getInsets
setName
toString
getPeer
preferredSize
stop
remove
remove
removeMouseMotionListener
removeComponentListener
getParameter
getAppletInfo
hide
size
removeAll
getMaximumSize
repaint
setStub
removeFocusListener
add
equals
DoYouKnowWhosOnThird
getFont
getAudioClip
start
setSize
removeContainerListener
gotFocus
resize
repaint
whatShouldBeOnSecond
add
getGraphics
addMouseListener
printAll
mouseExit
insets
getLocationOnScreen
getAppletContext
reshape
inside
```

```
whatIsOnSecond
removeMouseListener
mouseEnter
getComponentCount
add
deliverEvent
isAncestorOf
nextFocus
prepareImage
contains
getComponent
outputPD
printComponents
init
minimumSize
fattenPath
isShowing
enable
locate
addContainerListener
createImage
getImage
getSize
setBackground
getLayout
getBounds
addNotify
checkImage
notify
contains
getDocumentBase
lostFocus
show
disable
isVisible
keyUp
getComponentAt
setVisible
getComponentAt
setFont
addComponentListener
countComponents
setLayout
setBounds
notifyAll
```

```
location
paintComponents
setForeground
getImage
list
hashCode
getAudioClip
resize
getLocation
isEnabled
getColorModel
getToolkit
setEnabled
addKeyListener
requestFocus
list
layout
bounds
getParameterInfo
play
getClass
outputMD
mouseDrag
update
getMinimumSize
getTreeLock
add
validate
setSize
setBounds
repaint
setLocation
mouseDown
wait
paint
whoIsOnFirst
remove
mouseUp
mouseMove
list
removeKeyListener
postEvent
getName
add
destroy
```

```
getParent
checkImage
getCursor
prepareImage
paintAll
invalidate
imageUpdate
add
setLocation
LetMeTellYouWhosOnThird
keyDown
isValid
getAlignmentY
getAlignmentX
getFontMetrics
doLayout
setCursor
isFocusTraversable
transferFocus
play
getLocale
wait
dispatchEvent
list
getPreferredSize
getBackground
```

Core Reflection

The term "core reflection" means finding out information about the classes and methods at the core of a chunk of Java code. The basic methods that build a `BeanInfo` object use these core reflection methods to do the work. The methods will take names for classes and return information about all of the methods and patterns inside them.

To a large extent, the Core Reflection API is just a lower level approach to diving into a pile of code. Where the `BeanInfo` object comes with information bundled in the object from classes like `PropertyDescriptor` and `MethodDescriptor`, the information from the Core Reflection comes in objects from the classes `Field` and `Method`.

The main parts of the core reflection API are the classes `Class`, `Field`, `Method`, and `Constructor`. All except `Class` implement an interface known as `Member` that specifies some basic ways for looking at the information held in these classes. These four classes are part of the package `java.lang.reflect`.

Using the methods in the core reflection is not difficult, but it is somewhat grungy. Imagine that you're given an object and you want to know from which class it comes. One possible technique is to use the Java instruction `instanceof` and check all possible classes. This approach could fail if you miss a class.

The API offers another solution. The method `getClass` is part of the base class `Object` and it returns an item from the `Class` class. That is, it returns some information about the class of the object. In this case, the method `getName` will return a string with the name of the class. The method `toString` will also perform similar magic, but it will insert either the word "interface" or "class" before the name, depending on which is appropriate.

This is just one example of what you can do with the core reflection API. The tool becomes more powerful when you actually examine the parts of the class or create new versions of them.

Most people will not want to work with objects at this level. The tools they provide, though, are quite powerful. It is quite useful for code to examine other code because it makes it possible for programs to adapt to their surroundings. This is one reason why Java is much more an implementation of the great LISP tradition than the more scurrilous C tradition. Of course, some may feel otherwise.

The `Class` Class

Just talking about the `Class` class sounds confusing. But it is really just another object that contains information about the class itself. At least it seems to be.

In reality, it isn't a standard object. If you look for a public constructor, you won't find one. It's a primitive object that uses built-in methods to access the internal data structures. The methods like `getName` just access the low level data structures built up by the Java Virtual Machine when it loads the byte code. The class is really just a collection of methods that can peek at the lower level data.

This may seem like it could pose a security risk. At this time, there are no known security problems with letting other classes poke around at the definitions of an object. Only information marked "public" is released. The Java 1.1 security system adds another level of control—only signed applets are allowed to use the core reflection API to get at System classes.

Here are some of the methods in the `Class` class:

getName This takes no parameters and produces the "fully qualified name" of the object represented by the `Class` method. That is, a `String` with the package and the name of the class.

toString This produces a `String` with the name of the class. The beginning of the `String` contains either the word `class` or `interface`, depending upon which is appropriate.

forName(String) Pass in a string with the name of a class, and this will return the `Class` object if it is available.

getSigners This returns an array of `Object` representing the folks who signed this particular class file.

getSuperclass This is the next class up in the inheritence chain. You can use this to walk up the list of classes and find all of the methods. Sometimes a class merely inherits a method from a superclass and you need to climb this chain to find the method.

isInterface A boolean function that determines whether a given `Class` object represents a class that is really just an `interface`.

isPrimitive Some Java classes like `int`, `double`, and `boolean` are "primitive", which is to say that they're represented in memory with just a few bytes. They don't come with all of the `Object` overhead. This returns "true" if it is a primitive type.

isArray If the class is an array, then this returns true. So if you declare `Component[]` as the type of the variable `fred`, then `foo.getClass().isArray()` will return `true` and `foo.getClass().getName()` will return "Array". The method getComponentType will return the Class of the objects in the array. Notice that the word "Component" is used in two different ways here. They are not related. The Component class is part of the AWT.

getComponentType If the item is an array, then this returns the Class object describing the components of the array.

isInstance(Object) This is very similar to instanceof. For instance, foo.getClass().isInstance(foo) will always return true.

isAssignableFrom(Class) This takes a Class object and determines whether an object from that class can be assigned to a variable of that type. In other words, it checks to see if one class is a descendant of another. For instance, imagine that Foo is one class that is a direct descendant of Bar and foo and bar are objects from these respective classes. Then foo.getClass().isAssignableFrom(bar.getClass()) will produce true.

getField(String) This will look for a variable with the name in the String. It returns a Field object.

getDeclaredField(String) This will also look for a variable with the name in the String, but it will only look among the fields declared by this class file. That means avoiding the fields in the superclasses.

getFields() This produces an array of Field objects for all of the public fields accessible in the object.

getDeclaredFields() This also returns an array of Field objects, but it includes only the fields that are specifically declared by this class.

getInterfaces() This returns an array of Class objects containing the interfaces implemented by a Class. Note that if the object itself represents an interface, then this is a list of all of the superclasses of the Interface—that is, the other interfaces extended by the current one.

getMethod(String, Class[]) This will look for a method with the name in the String. It returns a Method object. The array of Class objects define the parameters that the method should take because there are often multiple versions of a method with the same name but different parameters.

getDeclaredMethod(String, Class[]) This will also look for a method with the name in the String, but it will look only among the methods declared by this class file. The array of Class objects define the parameters that the method should take because there are often multiple versions of a method with the same name but different parameters.

getMethods() This produces an array of Method objects for all of the public methods accessible in the object.

getDeclaredMethods() This also returns an array of Method objects, but it includes only the methods that are specifically declared by this class.

getContructor(Class[]) So you want a constructor for a class? Pass in an array of Class objects representing the parameters and this will search for one that fits your specifications. The result comes in the type Constructor.

getConstructors If you want an array with *all* of the constuctors, execute this one. Naturally, the objects in the array returned will be of the type Constructor.

getDeclaredContructor(Class[]) So you want a constructor for a class? You want to make sure that it was actually defined by a class and not inherited? Pass in an array of Class objects representing the parameters and this will search for one that fits your specifications. The result comes in the type Constructor.

getDeclaredConstructors If you want an array with *all* of the constuctors actually defined by a class file, execute this one. Naturally, the objects in the array returned will be of the type Constructor.

newInstance This will create a NEW object. It's sort of like running
the new command to a constructor with no parameters.

getModifiers A class may be public, abstract, or a host of other
things. This returns the modifiers as a 32-bit int. You'll need
to unpack them yourself. You can find the definition in the
documentation of the JVM. This is really low level Java hack-
ing.

Many of these methods behave similarly. If an array of length
zero comes back, it means that no methods or classes or whatever
are declared by this particular item. If you're asking for information
that can't be given, an exception like IllegalAccessException or
SecurityException will be thrown. There are also exceptions like
NoSuchFieldException or NoSuchMethodException and they mean
exactly what they say.

Here's some code that uses the getSuperclass method built into
the Class method.

```
package md12;
import java.awt.*;
import java.awt.event.*;
import java.applet.*;
import java.util.*;
import java.beans.*;
public class md12 extends Applet {
  public void chaseClassChain(Object o){
    // Walks up the chain of classes printing
    // out the class names.
    int depth=0;
    Class c=o.getClass();
    while (c!=null){
      for (int i=0;i<depth;i++){
        System.out.print(" ");
      }
      System.out.println(""+c);
        // Convert to string.
      depth++;
      c=c.getSuperclass();
    }
    System.out.println("------------");
  }
  //Initialize the applet
```

```
     public void init() {
       Object oo=null;
       oo=new Panel();
       chaseClassChain(oo);
       oo=new Button("Fred");
       chaseClassChain(oo);
       oo=new SimpleBeanInfo();
       chaseClassChain(oo);
       oo=new Applet();
       chaseClassChain(oo);
      }
     //Start the applet
     public void start() {
     }
     //Get Applet information
     public String getAppletInfo() {
       return "Applet Information";
     }
   }
```

The code, when run, generates this output:

```
class java.awt.Panel
 class java.awt.Container
  class java.awt.Component
   class java.lang.Object
------------
class java.awt.Button
 class java.awt.Component
  class java.lang.Object
------------
class java.beans.SimpleBeanInfo
 class java.lang.Object
------------
class java.applet.Applet
 class java.awt.Panel
  class java.awt.Container
   class java.awt.Component
    class java.lang.Object
------------
```

The Field Class

The `Field` class is a data structure and collection of methods that allow you to examine the contents of the different fields. If you execute the command `getFields` on a `Class` object, then you'll get an array of the objects from the `Field` class. These contain the information about the data fields in the object. You can use this information to do low level core reflection or to build up your own version of `BeanInfo`.

Most of the functions in the class involve reading or writing the actual data in the Field. So if, for instance, a field is a `Char`, then you can use the `getChar` function to get the contents and the `setChar` function to change them.

The access functions can throw either the `IllegalAccessException` or the `IllegalArgumentException`. The first comes when the "underlying field is inaccessible" and the second comes when "the field value cannot be converted into the return type by a widening conversion." A widening conversion happens when, for instance, a `short` is converted into a `long`.

Some of the other functions include:

equals(Object) Takes an object and sees if it "equals" another `Field` object.

get(Object) Let's say that `foo` is an item from the class `Field`. Let's say, for grins, that it is the variable "age" from the class `Person`. Further, let `fred` be an object from this class `Person`. You want to get the age of `fred`, so you execute `foo.get(fred)`, which will return an object containing the age.

If the age is primitive type, which it probably is, then you will get it in a wrapper class like `Integer`.

getBoolean ... getShort A function exists for each primitive type. That includes: `getByte`, `getChar`, `getDouble`, `getFloat`, `getInt`, and `getLong`. All of these take the object and produce primitive type data of the corresponding type. So `foo.getInt(fred)` will return an `int` version of the age of `fred`. If casting rules are violated, an `IllegalArgumentException` will be thrown.

setBoolean ... setShort There is one for each primitive type including `setByte`, `setChar`, `setDouble`, `setFloat`, `setInt`, and `setLong`. Let's say you want to set `fred`'s age to be 14; then you might execute `foo.setInt(fred,14)`. Each of these functions takes one target object and a value of the corresponding type.

set This is a more general version of the previous eight functions. It takes two arguments. The first is the target object and the second is an object with the value. If the types don't line up correctly and you shouldn't be stuffing an object of this type in this field, then an `IllegalArgumentException` will be thrown. If the field is inaccessible because it is `private` or something else, then an `IllegalAccessException` will be thrown.

getName For finding the name of the field. In the previous example, `foo.getName()` would return a `String` containing "age".

toString The same thing as `getName`.

getDeclaringClass This returns a `Class` object that represents the class that contains the `Field`. For instance, `foo.getDeclaringClass().getName()` would return a `String`, "Person".

[**getType**] This produces a `Class` of the type of the field. So if you execute `foo.getType()`, you would probably get something like the `Class` object for an `int` because that is the type used to store an age.

[**getModifiers**] This produces an `int` that encodes the different details about abstractness, finality, nativity, etc. You use this by executing code like `isPrivate(foo.getModifiers())`, which tells you whether the field representing the age is private or not. There are other boolean functions like `isAbstract`, `isFinal`, `isProtected`, `isStatic`, `isPublic`, `isSynchronized`, `isTransient`, or `isVolatile`. They all come from the class `Modifiers` and they also apply to the modifiers of the `Class` and `Method` objects.

Some Code Using the `Field` Class

This code searches through the fields for a few classic classes like
`Panel`, `SimpleBeanInfo`, `Button`, `Integer`, and `String`. The methods in the `Field` class are fairly powerful. You can look at the
information and you can even cast it into different classes if the rules
of Java allow the casting to occur. You can't probe the individual
bytes of an object with these tools.

There are two major functions here. The first, `plumbFields`,
will scan through the fields and use the `toString` function to print
out their values. The `get` method will pull out the object contained
inside the field in question.

The second function tries to use the more specific methods like
`getInt`, `getByte`, `getBoolean`, `getChar`, and `getFloat`. If these
can't get the right information out of the field, an `IllegalArgument-`
`Exception` is generated.

Note that nothing comes from probing the fields of `String`. There
are no accessible fields.

```
package MDField;
import java.awt.*;
import java.awt.event.*;
import java.applet.*;
import java.util.*;
import java.beans.*;
import java.lang.reflect.*;
public class MDField extends Applet {
  public void plumbFields(Object o){
    Class oc=o.getClass();
    Field[] ocf=oc.getFields();
    for (int i=0;i<ocf.length;i++){
      try{
        System.out.println(""+ocf[i]);
        System.out.println(" Value="+ocf[i].get(o));
      }  catch (IllegalAccessException e){
        System.out.println("Illegal Access Exception."+e);
      } catch (IllegalArgumentException e){
        System.out.println("Illegal Argument Exception."+e);
      }
    }
    System.out.println("=======");
  }
  public void allAccessAField(Field f, Object o){
```

```
      try{
        System.out.println(""+f.getBoolean(o));
        }   catch (IllegalAccessException e){
        System.out.println("Boolean: "+e);
        } catch (IllegalArgumentException e){
        System.out.println("Boolean: "+e);
      }
      try{
        System.out.println(""+f.getInt(o));
        }   catch (IllegalAccessException e){
        System.out.println("Int: "+e);
        } catch (IllegalArgumentException e){
        System.out.println("Int: "+e);
      }
      try{
        System.out.println(""+f.getFloat(o));
        }   catch (IllegalAccessException e){
        System.out.println("Float: "+e);
        } catch (IllegalArgumentException e){
        System.out.println("Float: "+e);
      }
      try{
        System.out.println(""+f.getByte(o));
        }   catch (IllegalAccessException e){
        System.out.println("Byte: "+e);
        } catch (IllegalArgumentException e){
        System.out.println("Byte: "+e);
      }
      try{
        System.out.println(""+f.getChar(o));
        }   catch (IllegalAccessException e){
        System.out.println("Char: "+e);
        } catch (IllegalArgumentException e){
        System.out.println("Char: "+e);
      }
  }
  public void deepPlumbFields(Object o){
    Class oc=o.getClass();
    Field[] ocf=oc.getFields();
    for (int i=0;i<ocf.length;i++){
      try{
        System.out.println(""+ocf[i]);
        allAccessAField(ocf[i],o);
        }   catch (IllegalAccessException e){
        System.out.println("Illegal Access Exception."+e);
```

```
    } catch (IllegalArgumentException e){
        System.out.println("Illegal Argument Exception."+e);
    }
  }
  System.out.println("=======");
}
//Initialize the applet
public void init() {
  Object o=new Panel();
  plumbFields(o);
  o=new SimpleBeanInfo();
  plumbFields(o);
  o=new Button("Hi");
  plumbFields(o);
  o=new Integer(1234);
  deepPlumbFields(o);
  o=new String("Hello");
  deepPlumbFields(o);
 }
//Get Applet information
public String getAppletInfo() {
  return "Applet Information";
}
}
```

The Output

```
public static final int java.awt.image.ImageObserver.WIDTH
 Value=1
public static final int java.awt.image.ImageObserver.HEIGHT
 Value=2
public static final int java.awt.image.ImageObserver.PROPERTIES
 Value=4
public static final int java.awt.image.ImageObserver.SOMEBITS
 Value=8
public static final int java.awt.image.ImageObserver.FRAMEBITS
 Value=16
public static final int java.awt.image.ImageObserver.ALLBITS
 Value=32
public static final int java.awt.image.ImageObserver.ERROR
 Value=64
public static final int java.awt.image.ImageObserver.ABORT
 Value=128
public static final float java.awt.Component.TOP_ALIGNMENT
 Value=0.0
```

```
public static final float java.awt.Component.CENTER_ALIGNMENT
 Value=0.5
public static final float java.awt.Component.BOTTOM_ALIGNMENT
 Value=1.0
public static final float java.awt.Component.LEFT_ALIGNMENT
 Value=0.0
public static final float java.awt.Component.RIGHT_ALIGNMENT
 Value=1.0
=======
public static final int java.beans.BeanInfo.ICON_COLOR_16x16
 Value=1
public static final int java.beans.BeanInfo.ICON_COLOR_32x32
 Value=2
public static final int java.beans.BeanInfo.ICON_MONO_16x16
 Value=3
public static final int java.beans.BeanInfo.ICON_MONO_32x32
 Value=4
=======
public static final int java.awt.image.ImageObserver.WIDTH
 Value=1
public static final int java.awt.image.ImageObserver.HEIGHT
 Value=2
public static final int java.awt.image.ImageObserver.PROPERTIES
 Value=4
public static final int java.awt.image.ImageObserver.SOMEBITS
 Value=8
public static final int java.awt.image.ImageObserver.FRAMEBITS
 Value=16
public static final int java.awt.image.ImageObserver.ALLBITS
 Value=32
public static final int java.awt.image.ImageObserver.ERROR
 Value=64
public static final int java.awt.image.ImageObserver.ABORT
 Value=128
public static final float java.awt.Component.TOP_ALIGNMENT
 Value=0.0
public static final float java.awt.Component.CENTER_ALIGNMENT
 Value=0.5
public static final float java.awt.Component.BOTTOM_ALIGNMENT
 Value=1.0
public static final float java.awt.Component.LEFT_ALIGNMENT
 Value=0.0
public static final float java.awt.Component.RIGHT_ALIGNMENT
 Value=1.0
=======
```

```
public static final int java.lang.Integer.MIN_VALUE
Boolean: java.lang.IllegalArgumentException: field type mismatch
-2147483648
-2.14748365E9
Byte: java.lang.IllegalArgumentException: field type mismatch
Char: java.lang.IllegalArgumentException: field type mismatch
public static final int java.lang.Integer.MAX_VALUE
Boolean: java.lang.IllegalArgumentException: field type mismatch
2147483647
2.14748365E9
Byte: java.lang.IllegalArgumentException: field type mismatch
Char: java.lang.IllegalArgumentException: field type mismatch
public static final java.lang.Class java.lang.Integer.TYPE
Boolean: java.lang.IllegalArgumentException: field type mismatch
Int: java.lang.IllegalArgumentException: field type mismatch
Float: java.lang.IllegalArgumentException: field type mismatch
Byte: java.lang.IllegalArgumentException: field type mismatch
Char: java.lang.IllegalArgumentException: field type mismatch
=======
```

The Method Class

The Method class is used to describe the various methods that are built into a Class object. Most of the functions for manipulating Method objects (yes, they're called methods too) are similar to the functions for manipulating Field objects because both implement the Member interface. There are the functions like getName, equal, getDeclaringClass, and getModifiers that work in the same way as with Field objects.

The major difference is that you can actually fire off the methods behind the Method objects if you so desire. This LISP-like behavior can be quite useful in some self-referential programming. Most people may never use it, but it can be very useful in some situations where you want to assemble programs on the fly.

The new functions are:

getExceptionTypes This returns an array of Class objects because exceptions are just other objects. These are the ones that could be thrown out of an execution of the method.

getParameterTypes This is an array of Class objects which, as you might expect, list the parameters expected by this method.

getReturnType Another Class object. The data returned by the underlying method will be of this type.

invoke(Object,Object[] Let's say that clear is a method from the class DataType and clearDescript is the Method object that describes it. Let x be an object of type DataType. Then clearDescript.invoke(x,paramArray) will apply the clear method to the x object with parameters from paramArray.

Chapter 13 contains an example for probing the methods inside a class. It also returns the results from a variety of standard AWT objects.

The Constructor Class

A special version of the Method class is the Constructor class. It also implements the Member interface and offers all of the basic methods of Method except invoke. Its own version is newInstance, which takes an array of objects serving as parameters and produces a new object.

Using Core Reflection

The Java Bean team added core reflection and introspection to Java so someone out there could build tools like BeanBox—that is, a tool that would link together Beans on the fly. The tool would use the routines described in this chapter to analyze a Bean and discover what could be done.

Most Bean programmers won't need to use these tools. Most of us will just create a Bean and use the standard tools built by someone else. But that doesn't mean that the routines can be forgotten. Here are some reasons that might slip by:

- You are writing your own flexible program for generating BeanInfo. Obviously, you could build one with hard-coded responses for the various properties, methods, and events, but that wouldn't grow with your Bean. You can use routines like `this.getClass()` to do self-introspection.

- Your Bean wants to know whether another Bean supports a class of events. It can discover this by looking at the interfaces implemented by the other Bean's class.

- Looking for the correct method for changing a property. While these should be easy to find by name, that may not always be the case.

- Your new software Bean may be installed in a strange environment. You need to look around for items like printers or other devices.

Most of the code for manipulating the objects from the different `Member` classes is easy to write. You simply execute a function like `getDeclaredMethods` and then use a `for` loop to skim through it. The `equals` function can help you do the searching.

Here's an example:

```
try{
        Method[] m=fred.getMethods();
catch(SecurityException s) {
 // code to bounce out.
} catch (Exception e) {
 // More general code to leave.
}
for (int i=0; i<m.length;i++){
    if (findMe.equals(m[i].getName())){
      // Do something.
      }
 }
```

Conclusions

The `BeanInfo` class and the other lower level classes for doing core reflection are some of the more advanced techniques described in this book. Most programmers may never need to execute any of these functions even if they spend a lifetime writing Beans.

For the most part, the routines described in this chapter are big data structures. They report information about the inside of the Bean in complex detail. Most of the functions will do things like "get data structure A" or "get data structure B". There is not much analysis underneath the surface.

But the fact that they are merely tools for peering into the guts of another Bean (or good, old Java class) doesn't mean that there aren't a variety of different possibilities around. These methods when combined with the standard class names make it possible for programmers to work well with other Beans. The possibilities are great.

Here are the important lessons from this chapter:

- The terms "introspection" and "core reflection" mean to look inside a Bean to discover what methods and variables are available.

- This makes it easier to interface two Beans because they can examine each other's guts before deciding how to interface. For instance, one may look for a version of `setTheFont` before trying to change the font of a Bean.

- The `BeanInfo` class is a big data structure that reports all of the details about another class.

- Java will construct a `BeanInfo` structure for you automatically— if you follow the basic design rules when you name everything.

- You can also create your own code for building the `BeanInfo` structure. You may want to do this if you want to hide the existence of a method or give a method a strange name.

- You can also dig deeper by using lower level functions for identifying the `Class`, `Method`, or `Field` associated with each Bean. This are quite powerful tools.

Chapter 8

BeanBoxes and Meta-Tools

The main goal of Java Beans programming is making it easy for people to glue the Beans together. When Sun began the Beans movement, it created BeanBox as an example of the simple tool that they expect will come to dominate the Bean environment. This program lets you place the Beans in a box on the screen and connect up the Bean parts with events. It's a simple tool for taking simple Beans and building them into applications.

Using BeanBox is not particularly difficult. Still, I don't find it to be powerful enough to use for more complicated applications. In these cases, I like to glue the Beans together with source code in much the same way that the examples do it. Pure Java code is easier for me to use than a visual development tool. Others may feel differently.

This chapter has two fairly different goals. The first is to explain how BeanBox works with a simple example borrowed using Sun's tools. The second is to explain how you can extend your Bean to make it work better with BeanBox. You can add your own tools for changing the properties of a Bean and these are used by BeanBox to let the user edit the properties.

Using BeanBox

The BeanBox tool is written entirely in Java. To use it, you must install both the Bean Development Kit (BDK) and the Java Development Kit (JDK) from Sun. You can download the latest versions from Sun's Javasoft website (`www.javasoft.com`). After installing them, you must make sure the path is set correctly on your PC or workstation so that the Java interpreter will load on command.

The BeanBox has three windows. Figure 8.1 shows the three windows as they appear just after starting up the application. One, labeled "ToolBox", shows a list of the Beans that are available. The program found them by looking through the directory `jars` in the BDK. These JAR files contain the Beans and their classes. Some even contain multiple Beans.

The BeanBox assembles the information about the Beans through the process of Introspection and Core Reflection described in Chapter 7. The name and the icon, for instance, are found in the `BeanInfo` data structure produced through introspection. There are four possible icons that might come with this structure (like `ICON_COLOR_16x16`) and pointers to the various descriptors. In this case, the name in the list comes from the `getDisplayName` method executed for the `BeanDescriptor` data object that is built by introspection.

The main window in the center of the image is used for assembling the Bean. If you select one of the items from the menu in the "ToolBox" window, you can insert that Bean in the main window. This is a more complex process than you might imagine. BeanBox doesn't simply draw a rectangle or put some marker in the window to symbolize the Bean. It actually creates a new copy of the Bean and starts it working. The best way to understand this is to create a copy of the Juggler Bean or the Sorting Demo Bean. Both will start running as soon as they're created.

The third window is a property editor. When you select a Bean in the main BeanBox window, the property editing window will change to reflect the properties of this Bean. (Selecting may be difficult because the Beans are actually working. If you click a Button Bean in the middle, the mouse click will be passed through to the Bean

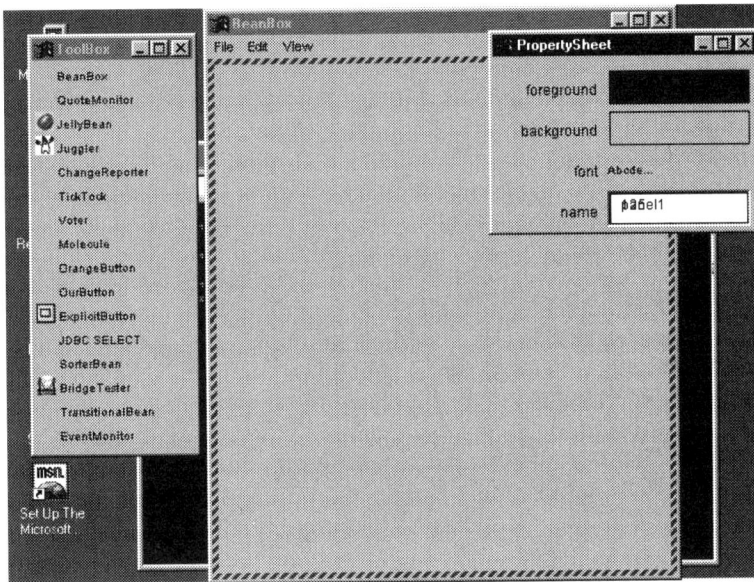

Figure 8.1: The first view of the BeanBox application after it has been fired up. The "ToolBox" window contains a list of Beans that are dropped into the main window and edited using the property editor window.

to depress the Button, *not* held by the BeanBox and interpreted to mean "select the Button now for editing".)

The BeanBox property editor is pretty smart. It looks at the types of the properties it finds through introspection and pops up a list. In this case, there are four properties for the main `Panel` used as a container for all of the Beans. Two of them are `Color`s, and the editor displays the actual color used for the foreground and the background. The `Font`, which isn't being used, is also displayed as it would be seen. The name of the panel is a `String`. If you click on one of the colored boxes, you can change the RGB values for the color or choose one of the standard colors. (The section beginning on page 152 describes how build your own custom editors if you need to do so.)

Figure 8.2 shows the BeanBox after a version of the Juggling Bean has been instantiated. It just sits there and juggles in its own separate thread.

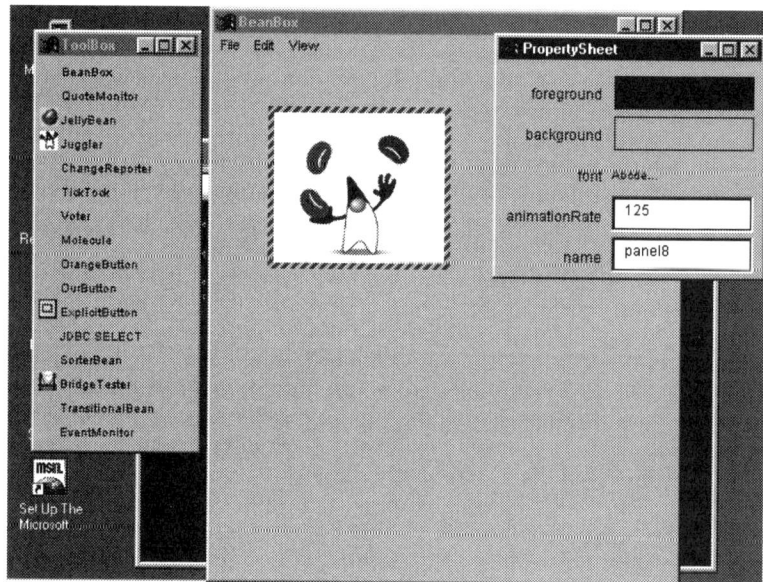

Figure 8.2: The BeanBox after one new Bean, the juggling Java thing, has been created. In real life, the Bean is actually moving after it is started. Paper can't recreate that effect.

The next step is to add several beans that will be used to control the juggling animation. The BeanBox comes with several button beans that have different levels of customizability. The one with the name `OurButton` has the most properties. Figure 8.3 shows the Bean-Box after two copies of these buttons have been instantiated and put in the `Panel` enclosing everything. The property editing window lets you change the `foreground`, `background`, `label`, `fontSize`, `font`, and `name`, as well as two boolean properties, `largeFont` and `debug`. Each of these properties comes from a standard set of types handled by the BeanBox so they don't use a custom property editor.

The BeanBox provides a way to link up the Beans graphically, but it is not particularly enlightening. The process takes several steps:

1. Select the Bean that will be generating an event. In this case it will be one of the buttons. This event is going to travel to the juggling bean to tell it to stop animating.

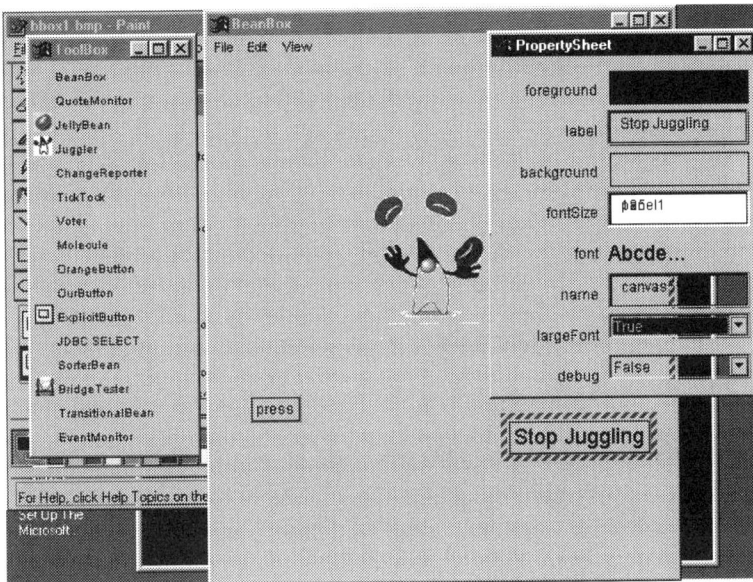

Figure 8.3: The BeanBox after adding two buttons. These buttons are quite customizable.

2. Go to the event menu item on the Edit menu. This will contain a list of the events generated by the Bean.

3. Select the Event "actionPerformed". Choosing the right event coming out of the Bean requires some knowledge of how the Bean performs. Ideally, the names will contain enough meaning to make it possible for an unfamiliar programmer to do the right thing. In practice, there will often be shades of gray and some experimentation may be necessary.

4. The BeanBox then starts drawing a red line that follows your mouse around. The goal is to identify the target or listener that will receive notice of the event. Other tools may use a different visual solution. Click on the juggler.

5. The BeanBox examines the `BeanInfo` record for the juggler and finds the methods that will accept an "actionPerformed" event. This list also includes the methods that take *no* parameters.

6. Select the method `startJuggling`. This is not a method in a class defined by a listener, but it does the right thing at the Bean. It will start the animation going.

7. The BeanBox generates a special event adapter class and compiles it. This is a listener of the right type for accepting an `actionPerformed` event that generates a method call of the right type. This allows everything to be bound together in a type-sensitive way.

If you arrange for the `actionPerformed` event from one button to trigger the `startJuggling` method on the animation and the other button's `actionPerformed` event to trigger the `stopJuggling` method, then you can have a working application. You can edit the names of the buttons to correspond to the actions.

It is also fun to arrange for the events from the buttons to go to multiple Beans. Figure 8.4 shows the BeanBox after a copy of the "Molecule" bean is added. This bean responds to a number of different events, but it makes public two methods for rotating the molecule around the X and Y axes. Although you can't tell by looking at the picture in the book, the `actionPerformed` events of the top button are routed to both the animating juggler and the molecule. The animating juggler starts juggling in response to the message and the molecule rotates a bit.

There are interesting side effects that become apparent. If you edit the `label` property of the button, it becomes obvious that each new letter added to the `label` will also generate an `actionPerformed` event. As I typed in "Start juggle and rotate", the molecule rotated after each keypress. This shows the wide variety of events that are generated and the need to be careful to understand the complete spectrum.

Customizing Classes

The BeanBox displays the list of each Bean's properties in a separate window. It contains the code for editing many of the basic types that will come along: numbers, colors, fonts, and strings. There will

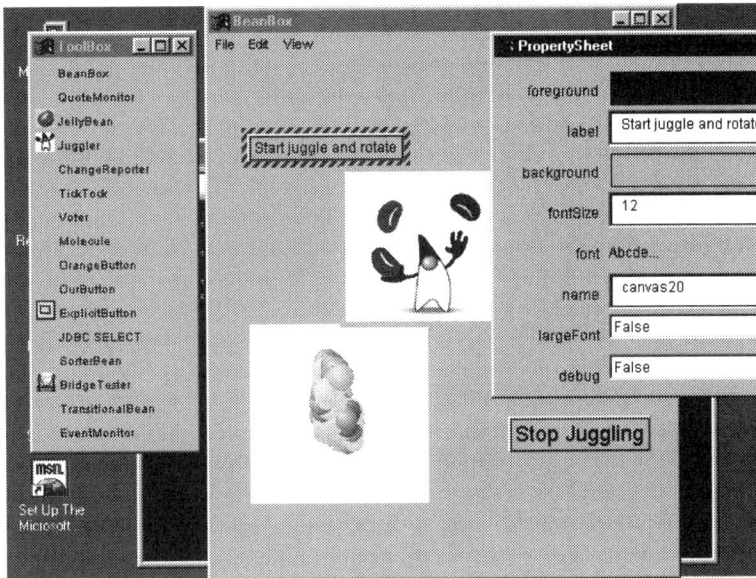

Figure 8.4: The BeanBox after adding two different beans controlled by two buttons. The top button will send an event to both the juggler and the molecule.

always be cases, however, that don't fit into these classes. This is why Sun provided the interface `PropertyEditor`. You can implement the interface and provide a way for people to edit your particularly weird property.

The interface for `PropertyEditor` is a pretty nice example of how to offer the user multiple levels of support. If your property is pretty simple, you can write only a few methods. If it is more complex, then you can add more methods that could build their own GUI for complicated tasks.

The job of a `PropertyEditor` is pretty simple. It interacts with a BeanBox-like bean editor through a set of standard methods and then it fires a `PropertyChangeEvent` to the bean after a new value is decided upon. Ideally, it will filter the new information to ensure that it is close to correct. In practice, the bean designers and the bean editor creators will probably be the same people and it is important that they balance where they place the code necessary to check for bad properties. Place only the necessary code in the Bean itself to reduce its size and leave the more general code in the editor.

The standard nomenclature is to name an editor for class "Foo" with the name "FooEditor". If you name it differently, then you must be prepared to generate your own `BeanInfo` data structure to inform the BeanBox which class will edit a type.

The `PropertyEditor` interface consists of the following methods. You don't need to implement all of them. In fact, the BeanBox looks to see which methods are available. If some aren't there, then it assumes that the property is simpler. If all are there, then it provides full support. Here are the methods you can subclass:

setAsText This is probably the simplest method and the most often implemented. It takes a `String` as a parameter and it must interpret the `String` to decide what to do to the property. That means if the `String` is "143.32" it might parse it into a `Double`. Or if the `String` is a file name, then it should look for the file and make sure it is available.

There are many creative ways to edit complicated properties with simple `String` values. One of the best is to provide a list of sample values with the `getTags` method. These are put in a pull-down menu by BeanBox and the user chooses one of them. For instance, the rotating molecule bean displayed in Figure 8.4 responds to the names of the chemicals to be displayed.

If the `String` is unacceptable, your version of this method should raise the `IllegalArgumentException`. This will be processed by the BeanBox to alert the user there is something wrong with the value passed in.

getAsText This takes no parameter but returns a `String` that represents the current value of the property. This `String` should be accepted by `setAsText`.

It is possible to implement only `setAsText` and `getAsText` as a minimal interface.

getTags This method takes no parameters but must return an array of `String`s containing the list of permissible items. If this method is implemented, the BeanBox will take the array and display it as a pull-down menu. This gives the user a limited number of choices for the property.

If you implement this method, you should make sure that `setAsText` will deal with all of the `Strings` in the array because it will have the job of accepting them.

It is a good idea to provide this list of possible values to the user. If you implement only `setAsText`, the user will need to make decisions on its own.

`setValue` How does your editor object learn about the property to be edited? It is passed in a copy through this method. Your version should take a general `Object` as a parameter but then quickly take it apart to determine the current values bundled inside.

It is important to clone the object immediately. A standard solution is to create a local variable of the right type and name it something like `target`. If you don't clone the object, you could write directly on the data of the object. This is pretty uncool. You can get away with it, but it messes up the data hierarchy. Any changes should be dispatched through the right `PropertyChangeEvents`.

Note: Primitive types like `int` must be wrapped up into `Object` descendants like `Integer`.

`getValue` This should return a version of the current object. It is the complement to `setValue`. It should return a value.

`isPaintable` Returns a `boolean` that expresses whether the current class will support the `paintValue` method.

`paintValue` This is a visual equivalent of `getValue`. It takes two parameters, a `Graphics` object and a `Rectangle`. You can draw anything you want in the `Rectangle` to illustrate the current value of the property. If it is a `Color`, then you might simply fill the rectangle with the corresponding RGB color. If it is a font, then you might draw it. These are standard types already handled automatically. You can use them for inspiration.

addPropertyChangeListener The BeanBox will call this routine with a list of objects that want to know about the property being changed. There will probably be only one. But you should maintain a local list. It takes the type PropertyChangeListener.

removePropertyChangeListener This removes it from the list.

getJavaInitializationString The BeanBox will occasionally create Java code and compile it. If you implement this method, then it should generate syntactically correct Java in a String. The Javasoft documentation gives examples like the string "2" or "new Color(127.127.34)". This code should sit on the right-hand side of an assignment statement.

You must implement this method.

getCustomEditor This takes no parameters and must return a Component. This Component can be anything that edits the current value of the property. If you don't implement this feature, just return a null value.

There are a number of details you must pay attention to. First, there must be some way for the Component to report the change. You should create the Component and arrange a link back to the PropertyEditor before ever returning a pointer with this method. Then, the Component can send a message to the PropertyEditor, which can fire off the right PropertyChangeEvent to the PropertyChangeListeners registered.

supportsCustomEditor This is a boolean function that should return true if the custom editor feature is built into getCustomEditor.

These are the different methods in the PropertyEditor interface. You don't need to support all of the methods, but you must support

some. The Javasoft documentation says that you must support one
of these three display options:

1. Produce an image through `paintValue`.

2. Produce a list of acceptable `String` values for inclusion in a
   menu by responding to `getTags`. You must also choose the
   current value from this array by returning it in response to a
   call of `getAsText`.

3. Produce a `String` from `getAsText`.

The BeanBox will use one of these three solutions to display the
current value for the user.

An Example

This is a simple example of a property that chooses one of five values,
in this case one of five types of fruit. The values are really an `int`,
but a series of constants is defined in the class `Fruit`. The value is
passed in and out of the `FruitEditor` class, however, in an `Integer`
wrapper. The interface demands a generic `Object` so the primitive
type of `int` won't do.

The rest of the system is fairly straightforward. The `getTags`
method sends out a list of the `Strings` containing the possible choices
and the `setAsText` inteprets the results. There is no image drawn,
although it would be cute to draw a picture of the right fruit. It isn't
hard to do.

One of the more interesting details in this implementation is that
there is no list of `PropertyChangeListeners` asking for notification.
There is only one. This is how the example written in the Sun documentation does it. You may want to be more circumspect and
implement the full support for a list of multiple listeners. This may
not be necessary now, but it may become necessary when a new generation of BeanBox-like tools emerge. They might register multiple
listeners.

```
import java.beans.*;
class Fruit {
  public static final int Pear=1;
```

```java
  public static final int Apple=2;
  public static final int Grape=3;
  public static final int Orange=4;
  public static final int Tomato=5;
  public static final String PearString="Pear";
  public static final String AppleString="Apple";
  public static final String GrapeString="Grape";
  public static final String OrangeString="Orange";
  public static final String TomatoString="Tomato";
}
public class FruitEditor implements PropertyEditor
{
  private PropertyChangeListener listener;
  private Object value;
  private int valueInt;
  public FruitEditor() {
     valueInt=Fruit.Pear;
     value=new Integer(valueInt);
  }
  public void setValue(Object o) {
    value = o;
    valueInt=((Integer)o).intValue();
    fire();
  }
  public Object getValue() {
    return value;
  }
  public boolean isPaintable() {
    return false;
  }
  public void paintValue(java.awt.Graphics gfx,
                         java.awt.Rectangle box) {
    // Nothing happens here.
  }
  public String getAsText() {
    String answer="";
    if (valueInt==Fruit.Pear){
      answer=Fruit.PearString;
    } else if (valueInt==Fruit.Apple){
      answer=Fruit.AppleString;
    } else if (valueInt==Fruit.Grape){
      answer=Fruit.GrapeString;
    } else if (valueInt==Fruit.Orange){
      answer=Fruit.OrangeString;
    } else if (valueInt==Fruit.Tomato){
```

```
      answer=Fruit.TomatoString;
   }
   return answer;
}
public String getJavaInitializationString() {
   // returns the one of the source code strings
   return (""+getAsText()+"");
}
public void setAsText(String text)
   throws java.lang.IllegalArgumentException {
   if (text.equals(Fruit.PearString)){
      valueInt=Fruit.Pear;
   } else if (text.equals(Fruit.AppleString)){
      valueInt=Fruit.Apple;
   } else if (text.equals(Fruit.GrapeString)){
      valueInt=Fruit.Grape;
   } else if (text.equals(Fruit.OrangeString)){
      valueInt=Fruit.Orange;
   } else if (text.equals(Fruit.TomatoString)){
      valueInt=Fruit.Tomato;
   }
   value=new Integer(valueInt);
}
public String[] getTags() {
   String ans[]= {Fruit.PearString,
                  Fruit.AppleString,
                  Fruit.GrapeString,
                  Fruit.OrangeString,
                  Fruit.TomatoString};
   return ans;
   }
public java.awt.Component getCustomEditor() {
    return null;
}
public boolean supportsCustomEditor() {
   return false;                        }
private void fire() {
   if (listener != null) {
     listener.propertyChange(
        new PropertyChangeEvent(this, "???", null, value));
   }
}
public void
 addPropertyChangeListener(PropertyChangeListener l) {
    listener = l;
```

```
  }
  public void
   removePropertyChangeListener(PropertyChangeListener l) {
    listener = null;
  }
}
```

JAR Files

Sun developed the JAR file standard to make it easier and faster to
distribute code. It is just an extension of the popular ZIP standard.
All of the pertinent `.class`, `.ser`, and `.GIF` files are compressed
together into one file. This makes transfer faster across the Web
because only one TCP/IP connection needs to be set up and torn
down. You can also add random text or data files into the mix if you
need to.

Many people often refer to the finished JAR file filled with all
of the various classes as the Bean itself. You're welcome to use the
term as you like.

In some cases, you'll have some decisions to make about whether
to include different files. The `FruitEditor` class is used by BeanBox
and you want it to be in the JAR file if the Bean is going to be
edited frequently. But if you are taking some serialized Beans and
sending them to do their job, you should leave out the editor files
like `FruitEditor`.

Conclusion

The BeanBox is one of the ends toward which Java Beans programming is aimed. If the Beans are well written, they should make all
of the relative events, properties, and methods available through the
`BeanInfo` data structure. The BeanBox lets you manipulate these
graphically.

While there are many reasons to be quite happy with the final
version of the BeanBox, there are other reasons to be frustrated.
The biggest I've found is that the names of the events aren't really
descriptive enough. I've had to go back to the source code to deter-

mine exactly what the events do before linking them up successfully. I think that text-based source code is still easier to use than graphical tools. Others will feel differently.

Never the less, I think that the Beans standard is quite powerful. Introspection can make it possible for all of us to write programs that pass around Beans and check their methods or properties. These dynamically defined programs can be quite powerful and useful.

Here's a list of BeanBox-like things you can do with Bean-like programming to act as inspiration:

- Create a translator program that accepts translation Beans for each language. It can test each language's Bean to see if it provides certain functions.

- Produce an extensible game system. Each character might be represented as a Bean. As time goes by, you might add more features and more weapons to the game. The process of introspection could be used to examine each character's Bean and determine which weapons and features were available.

- Build a dynamically linked food processing system. Each Bean would contain information and algorithms for cooking food. The computer-controlled ovens and mixing devices would poll the Beans to determine what methods needed to be invoked.

Chapter 9

An Example in Stereo

This example shows how to link two Beans with a vetoable property change. That is, if one Bean tries to change a property, another Bean has the ability to stop it in its tracks. In this case, the example includes two neighbors. One has a stereo (the `Volume1` Panel) and the other has a clock (the `NeighborClock` Panel). When the stereo wants to increase its volume, it sends a message to the `NeighborClock` asking permission. The `NeighborClock` determines what time it is and then makes a decision on the maximum permissible volume. If the volume is too large, then it throws a `PropertyVetoException`.

Here are some of the lessons to be learned from this example:

- You don't need to create your own event to deal with property change. You can use the structure here to send a message about the new time.

- You may want to create your own event and your own event interface. This is often recommended if you are going to have several different Beans listening for an event. In this case, the interface would extend `VetoableChangeListener`.

- This example uses some of the methods and classes created by Borland's JBuilder. This is an excellent product, but there is no reason why you can't use this example without the Borland classes. You just need to redo the layout functions of the `Applet`.

The `NeighborClock` Panel

```
package sound1;
import java.awt.*;
import java.awt.event.*;
import java.awt.Font;
import java.beans.*;
public class NeighborClock extends Panel
    implements VetoableChangeListener {
  Font drawFont;
  int hour=12, minute=0;
      // the time.    0 hour = midnight. 12=noon.
  Button plusHour, plusMinute;
  public int getHour(){
        return hour;
  }
   public int getMinute(){
        return minute;
  }
  public NeighborClock() {
    plusHour=new Button("Add Hour");
    plusMinute=new Button("Add Minute");
    add(plusHour);
    add(plusMinute);
    drawFont=new Font("TimesRoman",Font.PLAIN,24);
  }
  public void layout(){
     resize(100,300);
     if (plusHour!=null){
       plusHour.reshape(0,50,80,20);
     }
     if (plusMinute!=null){
       plusMinute.reshape(0,80,80,20);
     }
  }
  public void paint(Graphics g){
  g.setFont(drawFont);
   String drawMe=""+hour+":";
   if (minute<=9){
     drawMe=drawMe+"0";
   }
   drawMe=drawMe+minute;
    g.drawString(drawMe,4,28);
  }
  public boolean action(Event e, Object o){
     if (e.target==plusHour){
```

```
        hour+=1;
        if (hour >=24){
           hour=0;
        }
     } else if (e.target==plusMinute){
        minute+=1;
        if (minute>=60){
           minute=0;
           hour+=1;
           if (hour>=24){
              hour=0;
           }
        }
     }
     repaint();
     return true;
  }
public void vetoableChange(PropertyChangeEvent e)
 throws PropertyVetoException{
// Checks to see if it is too loud.
 int val=((Integer)e.getNewValue()).intValue();
 if (hour>21){
    if (val>4){
     throw new
       PropertyVetoException("Get some sleep.",e);
    }
} else if (hour <9){
    if (val > 5){
     throw new
       PropertyVetoException("Go back to bed.",e);
    }
} else if (val >10){
    throw new
       PropertyVetoException("Not to eleven!",e);
   }
  }
}
```

The Volume1 Panel

```
package sound1;
import java.awt.*;
import java.awt.event.*;
import java.beans.*;
```

```java
public class Volume1 extends Panel    {
  Button plusOne,minusOne;
  Label label1 = new Label("0");
  private int volumeValue=0;
  VetoableChangeSupport VC=
    new VetoableChangeSupport(this);
  public void
    addVetoableChangeListener
      (VetoableChangeListener l){
    VC.addVetoableChangeListener(l);
  }
  public void
    removeVetoableChangeListener
      (VetoableChangeListener l){
    VC.removeVetoableChangeListener(l);
  }
  public Volume1() {
    plusOne=new Button("+1");
    minusOne=new Button("-1");
    //this.add(scrollbar1);
    this.add(plusOne);
    this.add(label1);
    this.add(minusOne);
  }
  public void layout(){
    this.resize(100,150);
    plusOne.reshape(2,2,50,30);
    label1.reshape(2,55,30,30);
    minusOne.reshape(2,90,50,30);
  }
  public void tryChange(int i)
    throws PropertyVetoException{
    VC.fireVetoableChange("volume",
        new Integer(volumeValue),
        new Integer(volumeValue+i));
    int newOne=volumeValue+i;
    if ((newOne<=11) && (newOne>=0)){
      volumeValue=newOne;
    }
  }
   public boolean handleEvent(Event e){
      try{
        if (e.target==plusOne){
          tryChange(1);
          } else if (e.target==minusOne){
```

```
            tryChange(-1);
          }
        label1.setText(""+volumeValue);
        } catch (PropertyVetoException ee){
        }
      return true;
    }
}
```

The SoundMasterApplet Demo Applet

```java
package sound1;
import java.awt.*;
import java.awt.event.*;
import java.applet.*;
import borland.jbcl.layout.*;
import borland.jbcl.control.*;
public class SoundMaster1 extends Applet {
  XYLayout xYLayout1 = new XYLayout();
  boolean isStandalone = false;
  NeighborClock nc=null;
  Volume1 v1=null;
  //Get a parameter value
  public String getParameter(String key, String def) {
    return isStandalone ? System.getProperty(key, def) :
      (getParameter(key) != null ? getParameter(key) : def);
  }
  //Construct the applet
  public SoundMaster1() {
  }
  //Initialize the applet
  public void init() {
     v1=new Volume1();
     add(v1);
     nc=new NeighborClock();
      add(nc);
     v1.addVetoableChangeListener(nc);
  }
 public void layout(){
    this.resize(300,300);
    nc.move(0,50);
    v1.move(150,0);
  }
  //Get Applet information
  public String getAppletInfo() {
```

```
      return "Applet Information";
    }
    //Get parameter info
    public String[][] getParameterInfo() {
      return null;
    }
    //Main method
    static public void main(String[] args) {
      SoundMaster1 applet - new SoundMaster1();
      applet.isStandalone = true;
      DecoratedFrame frame = new DecoratedFrame();
      frame.setTitle("Applet Frame");
      frame.add(applet, BorderLayout.CENTER);
      applet.init();
      applet.start();
      frame.pack();
      Dimension d = Toolkit.getDefaultToolkit().getScreenSize();
      frame.setLocation((d.width - frame.getSize().width) / 2,
        (d.height - frame.getSize().height) / 2);
      frame.setVisible(true);
    }
  }
```

Chapter 10

Indicator Event Example

This chapter describes a more robust event passing example than the one found in Chapter 9. One of the more complicated problems for a programmer designing Beans is determining what sorts of events need a response. This is a deep design problem that has no absolutely correct solution. Some solutions are quicker and dirtier, while others are more likely to be useful to a wide variety of Beans users.

The problem is that no event mechanism can anticipate all of the different uses that people may want to put it to. This example glues together three different Beans that display values in three different ways. The first, `NumBean`, is just a numerical display that is a subclass of the AWT component `Label`. The second, `ThermBean`, is a thermometer-like bar display that fills up as the value grows. The third, `WarnBean`, shows a stoplight with red, yellow, and green lights. If the value reaches the danger zone, it turns yellow and then red.

Each of these three Beans is joined with Events. When `NumBean` gets a new value, it broadcasts a `PropertyChangeEvent` to everyone listening. This just happens to be the `ThermBean`. The `ThermBean`, in turn, generates a `PropertyChangeEvent`. This is captured by `WarnAdaptor`, a small class that acts as an event adapter to turn events into the type of events accepted by `WarnBean`.

This is a fairly complicated chain for a simple three-panel display, but it illustrates two different ways in which Beans should communicate. On one hand, `PropertyChangeEvent`s used by the first two Beans are very generic and easy to hook together. On the other, the WarnEvent accepted by the WarnBean is more descriptive but it requires an adapter to make it work.

The structure of these events is important because they determine how easy it will be for novice programmers to link the Beans together.

The NumBean Label

This Bean fires off a PropertyChangeEvent when it changes its value. This is the generic system built into the java.beans package to make it easier to notify other Beans of a simple change.

The biggest problem with this generic system is that it passes the new property as an object. In this case, the integer value is bound up in an Integer wrapper and it is unpacked on the other side of the line.

The only way to change the state of this Bean, however, is to execute the setTheState routine.

```java
package adapt;
import java.awt.*;
import java.util.*;
import java.awt.event.*;
import java.lang.*;
import java.beans.*;
  //PropertyChangeListener is here!
public class NumBean extends Label {
  int theState=0;
    // This is the temp;
   private PropertyChangeSupport
    ListenerList = new PropertyChangeSupport(this);
  public void setTheState(int a){
    int temp=theState;
    theState=a;
    this.setText(""+a);
    ListenerList.firePropertyChange(
      "newNum", new Integer(temp),new Integer(a));
  }
  public void addTheState(int a){
    setTheState(a+getTheState());
  }
  public int getTheState(){
        return theState;
  }
```

```
  public NumBean() {
    super();
  }
  public synchronized void
    addPropertyChangeListener(PropertyChangeListener l) {
    ListenerList.addPropertyChangeListener(l);
  }
  public synchronized void
    removePropertyChangeListener(PropertyChangeListener l){
    ListenerList.removePropertyChangeListener(l);
  }
}
```

The ThermBean Panel

This Bean is structurally not much different from the NumBean. It sends off PropertyChangeEvents when its state changes. The paint routine draws it as a bar.

The most noteworthy part of this Bean is the fact that it also accepts notification of PropertyChangeEvents. This is because it implements the interface PropertyChangeListener by providing a routine named propertyChange.

The structure of propertyChange may be a bit controversial. In this case, it accepts only events that come with the propertyName of "newNum". This feature makes it easier to control what it does, but it will also make it less useful. If you want your Beans to be more readily accepted by other Beans users, you should avoid putting too many conditions on the structure of the Bean coming in.

A better solution may be to add structure that tests the class of the object returned by getNewValue. In this case, it assumes it is a Integer. This works fine with this example, but it would fail if someone passed in something wrapped in a Double object. The more code you can add to adapt to the value, the more useful your Bean will be.

The downside is that your Bean will also grow fatter and it will take longer to develop. Eventually, every programmer must cut off the list of features. The structure of the propertyChange function is where there will be plenty of thinking about these quandaries.

```
package adapt;
```

```
import java.awt.*;
import java.util.*;
import java.awt.event.*;
import java.lang.*;
import java.beans.*;
  //PropertyChangeListener is here!
public class ThermBean extends Panel
        implements PropertyChangeListener{
  int thermState=0;
    // This is the temp;
  int thermMax=10000;
    // No minimum for this minimal example.
  private PropertyChangeSupport
    ListenerList = new PropertyChangeSupport(this);
  public void setThermState(int a){
    int temp=thermState;
    thermState=a;
    ListenerList.firePropertyChange(
      "newTherm", new Integer(temp),new Integer(a));
    repaint();
  }
  public int getThermState(){
        return thermState;
  }
  public void propertyChange(PropertyChangeEvent e){
    if (e.getPropertyName()=="newNum"){
      setThermState(((Integer)e.getNewValue()).intValue());
    }
  }
  public ThermBean() {
    super();
  }
   public void paint(Graphics g){
        // Write some stuff on the screen.
    Dimension d=this.size();
    g.setColor(Color.green);
    g.drawRect(0,0,d.width,20);
    int len=thermState/d.width;
    if (len>thermMax){
      len=thermMax;
    }
    g.setColor(Color.red);
    g.fillRect(0,0,len,20);
  }
  public synchronized void
```

```
    addPropertyChangeListener(PropertyChangeListener l) {
    ListenerList.addPropertyChangeListener(l);
  }
  public synchronized void
    removePropertyChangeListener(PropertyChangeListener l){
    ListenerList.removePropertyChangeListener(l);
  }
}
```

The WarnBean Panel

This is a small panel that displays three lights but lights up only one of them. This is a good tool for warning the user if values are getting out of the acceptable range.

This Bean, however, accepts events from the WarnEvent class. This custom-built class, described in the next section, is not widely supported. In this case, the Bean's programmer chose to create a special class of events that encapsulated the needs of the Bean— that is, show either a red, yellow, or green light.

The code beginning on page 175 shows what must be done to glue this Bean in with the ThermBean. The event adapter converts one into another with its own case statement.

```
package adapt;
import java.awt.*;
import java.util.*;
import java.awt.event.*;
import java.lang.*;
public class WarnBean extends Panel implements WarnEventListener{
  int lightState=0;
  static final int redState=2;
  static final int yellowState=1;
  static final int greenState=0;
    // This displays the right light.
  private Vector warnListenerList = new Vector();
  public void setLightState(int a){
        lightState=a;
        repaint();
  }
  public int getLightState(){
        return lightState;
  }
```

```
public WarnBean() {
  super();
}
 public void paint(Graphics g){
      // Write some stuff on the screen.
   g.setColor(Color.green);
  if (lightState==greenState){
      g.fillOval(1, 21,10,10);
  } else {
      g.drawOval(1,21,10,10);
  }
  g.setColor(Color.yellow);
  if (lightState==yellowState){
      g.fillOval(1, 11,10,10);
  } else {
      g.drawOval(1,11,10,10);
  }
  g.setColor(Color.red);
  if (lightState==redState){
      g.fillOval(1, 1,10,10);
  } else {
      g.drawOval(1,1,10,10);
  }
}
public void doWarning(WarnEvent e){
  switch (e.getID()) {
    case WarnEvent.goRed:  {
      setLightState(redState);
      break;
    }
    case WarnEvent.goYellow: {
      setLightState(yellowState);
      break;
    }
    case WarnEvent.goGreen: {
      setLightState(greenState);
      break;
    }
    }
  }
public synchronized void
  addWarnEventListener(WarnEventListener l) {
  warnListenerList.addElement(l);
}
public synchronized void
```

```
    removeWarnEventListener(WarnEventListener l){
    warnListenerList.removeElement(l);
  }
}
```

The WarnEvent Event

This is a custom-made event class for sending messages to the
WarnBean.   It defines three messages (goRed, goYellow, and
goGreen), which are stored as an integer inside the event.

```
package  adapt;
import java.util.*;
// This defines a new event, with minimum state.
public class WarnEvent extends EventObject {
  static final int goRed=2;
  static final int goYellow=1;
  static final int goGreen=0;
  private int id=0;
  public int getID() {return id;};
  WarnEvent(Object source,int i) {
    super(source);
    id=i;
    }
}
public interface WarnEventListener
  extends EventListener {
  public void doWarning(WarnEvent e);
}
```

The WarnAdaptor Event Adapter

The WarnAdaptor is an example of an event adapter written by a
programmer. Some event adapters are generated automatically by
tools like the BeanBox, but some require complicated code created
by a programmer. In this case, the code is just a simple if-then
block that converts a PropertyChangeEvent carrying a new integer
into the right color.

   One of the goals of Beans programming is to make it easier for
programmers to leverage each other's work. In this case, the event
adapter author didn't need to have any knowledge of the insides

of ThermBean or WarnBean. The information in the interface for
WarnEventListener was enough.

```
package adapt;
import java.beans.*;
import java.lang.*;
import java.util.*;
public class WarnAdaptor
  implements PropertyChangeListener {
  private Vector
    tellWhom=new Vector();
  public void propertyChange(PropertyChangeEvent e){
    if (e.getPropertyName()=="newTherm"){
      int temp=((Integer)e.getNewValue()).intValue();
      int newColor=WarnEvent.goGreen;
      WarnEvent we;
      if (temp>5000){
        newColor=WarnEvent.goRed;
      } else if (temp>1000){
        newColor=WarnEvent.goYellow;
      }
      we=new WarnEvent(e.getSource(),newColor);
      for (int i=0; i<tellWhom.size(); i++)
      //Send event to all registered listeners
        ((WarnEventListener)
          tellWhom.elementAt(i)).doWarning(we);
    }
  }
   public synchronized void
    addWarnEventListener(WarnEventListener l) {
    tellWhom.addElement(l);
  }
  public synchronized void
    removeWarnEventListener(WarnEventListener l){
    tellWhom.removeElement(l);
  }
}
```

The AdaptApplet Master Applet

This code is generated to illustrate how the Beans are joined together.
Some people who joined together three Beans might use a tool like
BeanBox to do the work, and that tool would generate something
similar to this.

There are several noteworthy parts of this example. The first is that the code is using the `instantiate` method to create the Beans. This method is pretty much a better choice than `new`. The `new` method is guaranteed to create an entirely new version from the `.class` file. The `instantiate` method will first look to see if there is a serialized version of the Bean available (i.e., one with a `.ser` suffix). If there is, it will deserialize it.

There are dangers with this approach. It uses the `instantiate` and then adds the connection. If any of these Beans are available on the disk, then the connection will be added again. Each event may be passed twice or more because the deserialized versions of the Beans will have versions of `ListenerList` or `tellWhom` with the old connections still in place.

The extra buttons, b1 and b2, are just used to test the Beans.

```
package adapt;
import java.beans.*;
import java.util.*;
import java.lang.*;
import java.awt.*;
import java.applet.*;
public class AdaptApplet extends Applet {
  NumBean nb;
  ThermBean tb;
  WarnAdaptor wa;
  WarnBean wb;
  Button b1,b2;
  public void init(){
    try {
      ClassLoader cl=AdaptApplet.class.getClassLoader();
      nb=(NumBean)Beans.instantiate(cl,"adapt.NumBean");
      nb.resize(120,30);
      add(nb);
      tb=(ThermBean)Beans.instantiate(cl,"adapt.ThermBean");
      tb.resize(200,40);
      add(tb);
      wa=new WarnAdaptor();
      wb=(WarnBean)Beans.instantiate(cl,"adapt.WarnBean");
      wb.resize(100,80);
      add(wb);
    } catch (ClassNotFoundException ce){
      System.out.println("Can't find the right class.");
    } catch (Exception e){
```

```
        System.out.println("Problems with this:"+e);
      }
      nb.addPropertyChangeListener(tb);
      tb.addPropertyChangeListener(wa);
      wa.addWarnEventListener(wb);
      b1=new Button("+1000");
      b2=new Button("-1000");
      add(b1);add(b2);
    }
    public boolean action(Event e,Object o){
      if (e.target==b1){
        nb.addTheState(1000);
        return true;
      } else if (e.target==b2){
        nb.addTheState(-1000);
        return true;
      } else {
        return false;
      }
    }
    public void layout(){
        if (nb!=null){
            nb.reshape(0,0,120,30);
        }
        if (tb!=null){
          tb.reshape(0,40,200,40);
        }
        if (wb!=null){
          wb.reshape(0,100,100,80);
        }
        if (b1!=null){
          b1.reshape(0,250,75,30);
        }
        if (b2!=null){
          b2.reshape(80,250,75,30);
        }
    }
}
```

Chapter 11

Self-Scrambling Example

This example is designed to show how to write your own code for controlling how a Bean serializes itself. In this case, the example ScramBean scrambles the data using a fairly rudimentary cipher. It unscrambles itself when it is loaded back in. The work is done by the readObject and writeObject.

The ScramApplet for Example

```
package scram;
import java.awt.*;
import java.awt.event.*;
import java.applet.*;
public class ScramApp1 extends Applet {
    boolean isStandalone = false;
    ScramBean sb;
  //Initialize the applet
  public void init() {
    try { jbInit(); }
      catch (Exception e)
    { e.printStackTrace(); }
  }
  //Component initialization
  public void jbInit() throws Exception{
```

```
        sb=new ScramBean();
        add(sb);
    }
    //Get Applet information
    public String getAppletInfo() {
      return "I'm a shell";
    }
    //Get parameter info
    public String[][] getParameterInfo() {
      return null;
    }
}
```

The ScramBean

```
package  scram;
import java.awt.*;
import java.awt.event.*;
import java.io.*;
import java.util.*;
public class ScramBean extends Panel
    implements Serializable{
  transient TextArea ta=null;
    // This will hold the data.
  byte[]  scramString=null;
    // This will hold the data during persistence.
  public ScramBean() {
    try {
      jbInit();
    }
    catch (Exception e) {
      e.printStackTrace();
    }
  }
  public void jbInit() throws Exception{
    ta=new TextArea("");
    this.add(ta);
```

```java
    }
    public void setText(String s) {
      ta.setText(s);
    }
    public String getText(){
      return ta.getText();
    }
    public void writeObject(ObjectOutputStream s)
        throws IOException{
      // This  scrambles the text.
      if (ta!=null){
        scramString=ta.getText().getBytes();
        ta.setText("");
          /// Clear it out.
        byte mask=(byte)255;
        for (int i=0;i<scramString.length;i++){
         scramString[i]=(byte)(scramString[i] ^ mask);
        }
      }
      s.defaultWriteObject();
    }
    public void readObject(ObjectInputStream s)
      throws IOException,ClassNotFoundException{
      // This descrambles the text.
      s.defaultReadObject();
      byte mask=(byte)255;
      for (int i=0;i<scramString.length;i++){
        scramString[i]=(byte)(scramString[i] ^ mask);
      }
      if (ta==null){
        ta= new TextArea(new String(scramString));
      } else {
        ta.setText(new String(scramString));
      }
    }
  }
}
```

Chapter 12

A Big Event Example

This chapter shows a large example designed to explore linking together many different Beans. In this case, there are four Beans, which are descended from the class `Panel`: `BoingPanel1`, `CartPanel1`, `DogPanel1`, and `TriPanel1`. None of them do much except draw some colored lines or shapes. The purpose of this example is to show how to use events to link up the different Panels.

In this example, there are two main classes of events: `AlphaBeatEvent` and `BetaBeatEvent`. Both conform to the Java Beans standard for naming by ending with the suffix `Event`. These two events are just carriers for an integer value, which in these cases is specified by a set of constants defined in the event. The events don't really do much except change the colors and the shapes displayed by the different `Panels`.

The most interesting part of this exercise may be the introspection and core reflection used by the main `Applet`, javaTreeApp1. This display shell creates 16 random `Panels` from the four possible classes and then checks to see what events they accept. Some panels accept only `AlphaBeatEvents`, some accept `BetaBeatEvents`, and some accept both. There are two routines, `testForAlphaBeat` and `testForBetaBeat`. The first uses the relatively low-level routine `getInterfaces` to find all of the different classes implemented by the `Panel` in question. The second creates the entire `BeanInfo` data structure and uses that to look for an implementation. Clearly, the first is more efficient if you're going to be looking for only one interface. The second is a better approach if you're going to be looking at other parts of a Bean as well.

The TreeApp Applet

```
package tree1;
import java.awt.*;
import java.awt.event.*;
import java.applet.*;
import java.beans.*;
import java.util.*;
public class TreeApp1 extends Applet {
  boolean isStandalone = false;
  private Vector listenerList = new Vector();
  private Vector betaListenerList = new Vector();
  Button But1,But2,But3,But4;
   TriPanel1 tp=null;
   BoingPanel1 bp=null;
   CartPanel1 cp=null;
   DogPanel1 dp=null;
  //Construct the applet
  public TreeApp1() {
  }
  public Panel chooseRandomPanel(){
    int num=new Double(4*Math.random()).intValue();
    if (num==0){
      return new TriPanel1();
    } else if (num==1){
      return new BoingPanel1();
    } else if (num==2){
      return new CartPanel1();
    } else {
      return new DogPanel1();
    }
  }
  public void loadLayoutPage(int max){
    Panel p=null;
     for (int i=0;i<max;i++){
       p=chooseRandomPanel();
       add(p);
       if (testForAlphaBeat(p)){
         addAlphaBeatEventListener(p);
       }
       if (testForBetaBeat(p)){
```

```
          addBetaBeatEventListener(p);
        }
      }
    }
    //Initialize the applet
    public void init() {
      setLayout(new GridLayout(4,5,2,2));
      loadLayoutPage(4*4);
      add(But1=new Button("AlphaBeat 1"));
      add(But2=new Button("AlphaBeat 2"));
      add(But3=new Button("BetaBeat 1"));
      add(But4=new Button("BetaBeat 2"));
    }
    public boolean testForAlphaBeat(Object o){
      boolean answer=false;
      try{
        Class oC=o.getClass();
        Class whatImplemented[] = oC.getInterfaces();
        Class lookForMe=
           Class.forName("tree1.AlphaBeatEventListener");
        for (int i=0; i<whatImplemented.length;i++){
          if (whatImplemented[i].equals(lookForMe)){
            answer=true;
          }
        }
      } catch (ClassNotFoundException e){
        System.out.println("Class not found exception.");
      } catch (Exception e){
        System.out.println("Another exception:"+e);
      }
      return answer;
    }
    public boolean testForBetaBeat(Object o){
    // Use BeanInfo to test for the BetaBeat events.
      boolean answer=false;
      Class oC=o.getClass();
      try{
        BeanInfo oBI=Introspector.getBeanInfo(oC);
        EventSetDescriptor[]
          oESD=oBI.getEventSetDescriptors();
        for (int i=0;i<oESD.length;i++){
          if(oESD[i].getName().equals("betaBeatEvent")){
            answer=true;
          }
        }
```

```
      } catch (IntrospectionException e){
        System.out.println("Introspection Exception:"+e);
      }
      return answer;
    }
  public boolean action(Event e, Object o){
    boolean answer=true;
    if (e.target==But1){
      processAlphaBeatEvent(
        new AlphaBeatEvent(this,AlphaBeatEvent.AlphaBeat1));
    } else if (e.target==But2){
      processAlphaBeatEvent(
        new AlphaBeatEvent(this,AlphaBeatEvent.AlphaBeat2));
    } else if (e.target==But3){
      processBetaBeatEvent(
        new BetaBeatEvent(this,BetaBeatEvent.EhEvent1));
    } else if (e.target==But4){
    } else {
      answer=false;
    }
    repaint();
    return answer;
  }
  //Get Applet information
  public String getAppletInfo() {
    return "Applet Information";
  }
  //Get parameter info
  public String[][] getParameterInfo() {
    return null;
  }
  public synchronized void
    addAlphaBeatEventListener(Object l) {
    listenerList.addElement(l);
  }
  public synchronized void
    removeAlphaBeatEventListener(AlphaBeatEventListener l){
    listenerList.removeElement(l);
  }
   protected void processAlphaBeatEvent(AlphaBeatEvent e) {
    switch (e.getID()) {
      case AlphaBeatEvent.AlphaBeat1:
        for (int i=0; i<listenerList.size(); i++)
          //Send event to all registered listeners
          ((AlphaBeatEventListener)
```

```
          listenerList.elementAt(i)).doAlphaBeat1(e);
        break;
      case AlphaBeatEvent.AlphaBeat2:
        for (int i=0; i<listenerList.size(); i++)
          ((AlphaBeatEventListener)
            listenerList.elementAt(i)).doAlphaBeat2(e);
        break;
    }
  }
  public synchronized void
    addBetaBeatEventListener(Object l) {
    betaListenerList.addElement(l);
  }
  public synchronized void
    removeBetaBeatEventListener(BetaBeatEventListener l){
    betaListenerList.removeElement(l);
  }
  protected void processBetaBeatEvent(BetaBeatEvent e) {
    switch (e.getID()) {
      case BetaBeatEvent.EhEvent1:
        for (int i=0; i<betaListenerList.size(); i++)
          //Send event to all registered listeners
          ((BetaBeatEventListener)
            betaListenerList.elementAt(i)).doEhEvent(e);
        break;
      case BetaBeatEvent.BeeEvent2:
        for (int i=0; i<betaListenerList.size(); i++)
          ((BetaBeatEventListener)
            betaListenerList.elementAt(i)).doBeeEvent(e);
        break;
      case BetaBeatEvent.SeeEvent3:
        for (int i=0; i<betaListenerList.size(); i++)
          ((BetaBeatEventListener)
            betaListenerList.elementAt(i)).doSeeEvent(e);
        break;
    }
  }
}
```

The AlphaBeatEvent Event

```
package  tree1;
import java.util.*;
// This defines a new event, with minimum state.
```

```
public class AlphaBeatEvent extends EventObject {
  static final int AlphaBeat1=1;
  static final int AlphaBeat2=2;
  private int id=0;
  public int getID() {return id;};
  AlphaBeatEvent(Object source,int i) {
    super(source);
    id=i;
    }
}
// This defines a listener
// interface for the set of events that
// are generated by AlphaBeatEvent
public interface
  AlphaBeatEventListener extends EventListener {
   public void doAlphaBeat1(AlphaBeatEvent e);
   public void doAlphaBeat2(AlphaBeatEvent e);
}
```

The BetaBeatEvent Event

```
%%% BetaBeat
package  tree1;
import java.util.*;
// This defines a new event,
// with minimum state.
public class BetaBeatEvent extends EventObject {
  static final int EhEvent1=1;
  static final int BeeEvent2=2;
  static final int SeeEvent3=3;
  private int id=0;
  public int getID() {return id;};
  BetaBeatEvent(Object source,int i) {
    super(source);
    id=i;
    }
}
// This defines a listener
// interface for the set of events that
// are generated by BetaBeatEvent.
public interface
  BetaBeatEventListener extends EventListener {
   public void doEhEvent(BetaBeatEvent e);
   public void doBeeEvent(BetaBeatEvent e);
```

```
    public void doSeeEvent(BetaBeatEvent e);
}
```

The BoingPanel1 Panel

```
package tree1;
import java.awt.*;
import java.util.*;
import java.awt.event.*;
public class BoingPanel1 extends Panel
    implements AlphaBeatEventListener, BetaBeatEventListener{
  int lightState=0;
  int inverseState=0;
  private Vector listenerList = new Vector();
  private Vector betaListenerList = new Vector();
  public void setLightState(int a){
        lightState=a;
  }
  public int getLightState(){
        return lightState;
  }
  public void cycleLightState(){
        lightState++;
        if (lightState>3){
            lightState=0;
        }
  }
  public BoingPanel1() {
    super();
  }
  public void paint(Graphics g){
        // Write some stuff on the screen.
    if (lightState==0){
        g.setColor(Color.magenta);
    } else if (lightState==1){
        g.setColor(Color.cyan);
    } else {
        g.setColor(Color.orange);
    }
    if (inverseState==0){
        g.fillRect(5, 5,15,15);
    } else if (inverseState==1){
        g.fillRect(20,5,15,15);
    } else if (inverseState==2){
```

```
      g.fillRect(5,20,15,15);
    } else if (inverseState==3){
      g.fillRect(20,20,15,15);
    } else if (inverseState==4){
      g.fillRect(5,5,15,15);
      g.fillRect(20,20,15,15);
    } else if (inverseState==5){
      g.fillRect(20,5,15,15);
      g.fillRect(5,20,15,15);
    } else if (inverseState==6){
      g.fillRect(5,5,15,15);
      g.fillRect(5,20,15,15);
      g.fillRect(20,5,15,15);
    } else if (inverseState==7){
      g.fillRect(5,20,15,15);
      g.fillRect(20,5,15,15);
      g.fillRect(20,20,15,15);
    }
  }
  public void doEhEvent(BetaBeatEvent e){
    inverseState+=3;
    if (inverseState>=8){
      inverseState-=8;
    }
    repaint();
  }
  public void doBeeEvent(BetaBeatEvent e){
    inverseState+=1;
    if (inverseState>=8){
      inverseState-=8;
    }
    repaint();
  }
    public void doSeeEvent(BetaBeatEvent e){
    inverseState+=1;
    if (inverseState>=8){
      inverseState-=8;
    }
    repaint();
  }
  public void doAlphaBeat1(AlphaBeatEvent e){
        if (lightState==2){
          lightState=0;
        } else {
          lightState++;
```

```
        }
     repaint();
   }
  public void doAlphaBeat2(AlphaBeatEvent e){
         if (lightState==0){
           lightState=1;
         } else {
           lightState--;
         }
     repaint();
   }
public synchronized void
 addBetaBeatEventListener(BetaBeatEventListener l) {
        betaListenerList.addElement(l);
   }
public synchronized void
 removeBetaBeatEventListener(BetaBeatEventListener l){
    betaListenerList.removeElement(l);
   }
 protected void processBetaBeatEvent(BetaBeatEvent e) {
   switch (e.getID()) {
    case BetaBeatEvent.EhEvent1:
     for (int i=0; i<betaListenerList.size(); i++)
      //Send event to all registered listeners
       ((BetaBeatEventListener)
         betaListenerList.elementAt(i)).doEhEvent(e);
       break;
    case BetaBeatEvent.BeeEvent2:
     for (int i=0; i<betaListenerList.size(); i++)
        ((BetaBeatEventListener)
          betaListenerList.elementAt(i)).doBeeEvent(e);
      break;
    case BetaBeatEvent.SeeEvent3:
     for (int i=0; i<betaListenerList.size(); i++)
        ((BetaBeatEventListener)
          betaListenerList.elementAt(i)).doSeeEvent(e);
      break;
  }
}
public synchronized void
  addAlphaBeatEventListener(AlphaBeatEventListener l) {
   listenerList.addElement(l);
}
public synchronized void
 removeAlphaBeatEventListener(AlphaBeatEventListener l){
```

```
      listenerList.removeElement(l);
}
protected void processAlphaBeatEvent(AlphaBeatEvent e) {
 switch (e.getID()) {
  case AlphaBeatEvent.AlphaBeat1:
   for (int i=0; i<listenerList.size(); i++)
     //Send event to all registered listeners
     ((AlphaBeatEventListener)
       listenerList.elementAt(i)).doAlphaBeat1(e);
     break;
  case AlphaBeatEvent.AlphaBeat2:
    for (int i=0; i<listenerList.size(); i++)
      ((AlphaBeatEventListener)
       listenerList.elementAt(i)).doAlphaBeat2(e);
        break;
 }
 }
}
```

The CartPanel1 Panel

```
package tree1;
import java.awt.*;
import java.util.*;
import java.awt.event.*;
import java.lang.*;
public class CartPanel1 extends Panel
    implements AlphaBeatEventListener,
               BetaBeatEventListener{
  int lightState=0;
  int inverseState=3;
  private Vector listenerList = new Vector();
  private Vector betaListenerList = new Vector();
  public void setLightState(int a){
        lightState=a;
  }
  public int getLightState(){
        return lightState;
  }
  public CartPanel1() {
    super();
  }
   public void paint(Graphics g){
        // Write some stuff on the screen.
```

```
  if (lightState==0){
     g.setColor(Color.red);
  } else if (lightState==1){
     g.setColor(Color.blue);
  } else {
     g.setColor(Color.green);
  }
  int y=0;
  for (int i=0;i<30;i++){
    g.drawLine(2,y,40,y);
    y+=inverseState;
    if (y>=40){
      y-=40;
    }
  }
}
public void doEhEvent(BetaBeatEvent e){
   if (inverseState==3){
     inverseState=7;
   } else if (inverseState==7){
     inverseState=9;
   } else if (inverseState==9){
     inverseState=3;
   } else  {
     inverseState=3;
   }
   repaint();
}
public void doBeeEvent(BetaBeatEvent e){
   inverseState+=1;
   if (inverseState>=8){
      inverseState-=8;
   }
   repaint();
}
public void doSeeEvent(BetaBeatEvent e){
  inverseState+=lightState;
  inverseState+=1;
  if (inverseState>=8){
     inverseState-=8;
  }
  repaint();
}
public void doAlphaBeat1(AlphaBeatEvent e){
      if (lightState==2){
```

```
            lightState=0;
          } else {
            lightState++;
          }
      repaint();
    }
  public void doAlphaBeat2(AlphaBeatEvent e){
          if (lightState==0){
            lightState=1;
          } else {
            lightState--;
          }
      repaint();
    }
public synchronized void
  addBetaBeatEventListener(BetaBeatEventListener l) {
  betaListenerList.addElement(l);
}
public synchronized void
  removeBetaBeatEventListener(BetaBeatEventListener l){
  betaListenerList.removeElement(l);
}
protected void processBetaBeatEvent(BetaBeatEvent e) {
 switch (e.getID()) {
  case BetaBeatEvent.EhEvent1:
   for (int i=0; i<betaListenerList.size(); i++)
    //Send event to all registered listeners
    ((BetaBeatEventListener)
    betaListenerList.elementAt(i)).doEhEvent(e);
    break;
  case BetaBeatEvent.BeeEvent2:
   for (int i=0; i<betaListenerList.size(); i++)
    ((BetaBeatEventListener)
     betaListenerList.elementAt(i)).doBeeEvent(e);
    break;
  case BetaBeatEvent.SeeEvent3:
   for (int i=0; i<betaListenerList.size(); i++)
    ((BetaBeatEventListener)
     betaListenerList.elementAt(i)).doSeeEvent(e);
    break;
  }
}
public synchronized void
 addAlphaBeatEventListener(AlphaBeatEventListener l) {
  listenerList.addElement(l);
```

```
 }
public synchronized void
 removeAlphaBeatEventListener(AlphaBeatEventListener l){
   listenerList.removeElement(l);
}
protected void processAlphaBeatEvent(AlphaBeatEvent e) {
 switch (e.getID()) {
   case AlphaBeatEvent.AlphaBeat1:
    for (int i=0; i<listenerList.size(); i++)
      //Send event to all registered listeners
     ((AlphaBeatEventListener)
        listenerList.elementAt(i)).doAlphaBeat1(e);
     break;
   case AlphaBeatEvent.AlphaBeat2:
    for (int i=0; i<listenerList.size(); i++)
     ((AlphaBeatEventListener)
       listenerList.elementAt(i)).doAlphaBeat2(e);
    break;
   }
  }
}
```

The DogPanel1 Panel

```
package tree1;
import java.awt.*;
import java.util.*;
import java.awt.event.*;
import java.lang.*;
public class DogPanel1 extends Panel
   implements BetaBeatEventListener{
  int lightState=0;
  int inverseState=3;
  private Vector betaListenerList = new Vector();
  public void setLightState(int a){
        lightState=a;
  }
  public int getLightState(){
        return lightState;
  }
  public DogPanel1() {
    super();
  }
   public void paint(Graphics g){
```

```
      // Write some stuff on the screen.
  if (lightState==0){
     g.setColor(Color.orange);
  }  else if (lightState==1){
     g.setColor(Color.magenta);
  } else {
     g.setColor(Color.yellow);
  }
  int y=0;
  for (int i=0;i<7;i++){
    g.fillRect(2,y,30+i,2);
    y+=inverseState;
    if (y>=40){
      y-=40;
    }
  }
}
public void doEhEvent(BetaBeatEvent e){
   if (inverseState==3){
     inverseState=7;
   } else if (inverseState==7){
     inverseState=9;
   } else if (inverseState==9){
     inverseState=3;
   } else  {
     inverseState=3;
   }
   repaint();
}
public void doBeeEvent(BetaBeatEvent e){
   inverseState+=1;
   if (inverseState>=8){
      inverseState-=8;
   }
   repaint();
}
public void doSeeEvent(BetaBeatEvent e){
  inverseState+=lightState;
  inverseState+=1;
  if (inverseState>=8){
     inverseState-=8;
  }
  repaint();
}
// The add/remove methods provide
```

```
  // the signature for the IDE to recognize
  // these events and show them in the event list
public synchronized void
 addBetaBeatEventListener(BetaBeatEventListener l) {
  betaListenerList.addElement(l);
}
public synchronized void
 removeBetaBeatEventListener(BetaBeatEventListener l){
 betaListenerList.removeElement(l);
}
  // A single process method keeps
  // all event dispatching in one place.
  // Separate processEVENT1, processEVENT2,
  // etc methods could also be used.
protected void processBetaBeatEvent(BetaBeatEvent e) {
 switch (e.getID()) {
  case BetaBeatEvent.EhEvent1:
   for (int i=0; i<betaListenerList.size(); i++)
   //Send event to all registered listeners
   ((BetaBeatEventListener)
     betaListenerList.elementAt(i)).doEhEvent(e);
     break;
  case BetaBeatEvent.BeeEvent2:
   for (int i=0; i<betaListenerList.size(); i++)
    ((BetaBeatEventListener)
      betaListenerList.elementAt(i)).doBeeEvent(e);
    break;
  case BetaBeatEvent.SeeEvent3:
   for (int i=0; i<betaListenerList.size(); i++)
    ((BetaBeatEventListener)
      betaListenerList.elementAt(i)).doSeeEvent(e);
    break;
  }
 }
}
```

The TriPanel1 Panel

```
package tree1;
import java.awt.*;
import java.util.*;
import java.awt.event.*;
public class TriPanel1 extends Panel
    implements AlphaBeatEventListener{
```

```
int lightState=0;
private Vector listenerList = new Vector();
public void setLightState(int a){
      lightState=a;
}
public int getLightState(){
      return lightState;
}
public void cycleLightState(){
      lightState++;
      if (lightState>2){
         lightState=0;
      }
}
public TriPanel1() {
  super();
  //resize(50,50);
}
 public void paint(Graphics g){
      // Write some stuff on the screen.
  if (lightState==0){
     g.setColor(Color.red);
  } else if (lightState==1){
     g.setColor(Color.blue);
  } else {
     g.setColor(Color.green);
  }
  g.fillOval(5, 5,40,40);
}
public void doAlphaBeat1(AlphaBeatEvent e){
      if (lightState==2){
         lightState=0;
      } else {
         lightState++;
      }
      repaint();
 }
public void doAlphaBeat2(AlphaBeatEvent e){
       if (lightState==0){
         lightState=1;
       } else {
         lightState--;
       }
       repaint();
}
```

```
public synchronized void
  addAlphaBeatEventListener(AlphaBeatEventListener l) {
  listenerList.addElement(l);
}
public synchronized void
  removeAlphaBeatEventListener(AlphaBeatEventListener l){
  listenerList.removeElement(l);
}
// A single process method keeps
// all event dispatching in one place.
// Separate processEVENT1, processEVENT2,
// etc methods could also be used.
protected void processAlphaBeatEvent(AlphaBeatEvent e) {
  switch (e.getID()) {
    case AlphaBeatEvent.AlphaBeat1:
      for (int i=0; i<listenerList.size(); i++)
        //Send event to all registered listeners
        ((AlphaBeatEventListener)
          listenerList.elementAt(i)).doAlphaBeat1(e);
      break;
    case AlphaBeatEvent.AlphaBeat2:
      for (int i=0; i<listenerList.size(); i++)
        ((AlphaBeatEventListener)
          listenerList.elementAt(i)).doAlphaBeat2(e);
      break;
  }
 }
}
```

Chapter 13

Digging Deep

The `BeanInfo` data structure is just the beginning. In many cases, you can't even get the information you need from the data structure itself. This example shows how you can find other information in adjoining data structures. For instance, if you try to look at the `ParameterDescriptor` values in each `MethodDescriptor`, you'll often find nothing. The generic `getBeanInfo` routine doesn't find anything. It places a `null` in this slot.

This example also shows the power of the `getBeanInfo` routine. This version uses a single parameter, the `Class` of the object for which the `BeanInfo` is desired. This means that it will dig up all of the possible methods available for the Bean. In this case, the Bean is a descendant of `Panel`, a class in the AWT that comes with a wide variety of inherited methods.

Another version of the `getBeanInfo` takes two parameters. The second specifies a `Class` where the search routine should stop climbing the chain of inheritance. This cuts the size of `BeanInfo` and saves time.

The `CountPanel` Panel

```
package md1;
import java.awt.*;
import java.util.*;
import java.awt.event.*;
```

```
public class CountPanel extends Panel{
  int count=0;
  int inverseState=0;
  public void setCount(int a){
        count=a;
  }
  public int getCount(){
        return count;
  }
  public void cycleCount(){
        count++;
        if (count>6){
           count=0;
        }
  }
  public CountPanel() {
    super();
  }
   public void paint(Graphics g){
        // Write some stuff on the screen.
    if ((count % 3)==0){
        g.setColor(Color.magenta);
    } else if ((count % 3)==1){
        g.setColor(Color.cyan);
    } else {
        g.setColor(Color.orange);
    }
    for (int i=0; i<count; i++){
      g.drawLine(0,2*i,40,2*i);
    }
  }
}
```

The Main Applet, TestMD1

```
package md1;
import java.awt.*;
import java.awt.event.*;
import java.applet.*;
import java.beans.*;
import java.util.*;
import java.lang.reflect.*;
public class TestMD1 extends Applet {
  Panel testCount=null;
```

```
BeanInfo cBI=null;
//Construct the applet
public TestMD1() {
}
public void printViaMethod(MethodDescriptor m){
 // Sometimes BeanInfo does a bad job.
 Method mM=m.getMethod();
 Class[] mc=mM.getParameterTypes();
 System.out.println(""+mM);
 System.out.print("   Parameter Types:");
 for (int i=0;i<mc.length;i++){
   System.out.print(" "+mc[i].getName());
 }
 System.out.println(" ");
 // Now look for return.
 Class ret=mM.getReturnType();
 if (ret!=null){
    System.out.println("   Returns:"+ret.getName());
 } else {
    System.out.println("   Returns: void");
 }
 Class[] md=mM.getExceptionTypes();
 System.out.print("   Exception Types:");
 for (int i=0;i<md.length;i++){
   System.out.print(" "+md[i].getName());
 }
 System.out.println(" ");
}
public void printMethod(MethodDescriptor m){
  ParameterDescriptor[] pd=m.getParameterDescriptors();
  if (pd!=null){
  // Returns NULL if nothing there!
     for (int i=0;i<pd.length;i++){
      if (pd[i]!=null){
       System.out.println("  "+pd[i].getName());
      }
     }
  } else {
    printViaMethod(m);
  }
}
public void doMethods(Object o){
  try{
    Class oc=o.getClass();
    // getBeanInfo requires a Class!
```

```
        cBI=Introspector.getBeanInfo(oc);
        MethodDescriptor[] md=cBI.getMethodDescriptors();
        for (int i=0;i<md.length;i++){
          System.out.println("Method:"+md[i].getName());
          printMethod(md[i]);
        }
      } catch (IntrospectionException e){
        System.out.println("Can't get the BeanInfo.");
      }
    }
  //Initialize the applet
  public void init() {
      testCount=new CountPanel();
      doMethods(testCount);
    }
  //Get Applet information
  public String getAppletInfo() {
    return "Applet Information";
  }
}
```

The Output

```
Method:isVisible
   Parameter Types:
   Returns:boolean
   Exception Types:
Method:locate
   Parameter Types: int int
   Returns:java.awt.Component
   Exception Types:
Method:enable
   Parameter Types:
   Returns:void
   Exception Types:
Method:getSize
   Parameter Types:
   Returns:java.awt.Dimension
   Exception Types:
Method:addNotify
   Parameter Types:
   Returns:void
   Exception Types:
Method:createImage
```

```
   Parameter Types: java.awt.image.ImageProducer
   Returns:java.awt.Image
   Exception Types:
Method:isFocusTraversable
   Parameter Types:
   Returns:boolean
   Exception Types:
Method:enable
   Parameter Types: boolean
   Returns:void
   Exception Types:
Method:location
   Parameter Types:
   Returns:java.awt.Point
   Exception Types:
Method:addContainerListener
   Parameter Types: java.awt.event.ContainerListener
   Returns:void
   Exception Types:
Method:size
   Parameter Types:
   Returns:java.awt.Dimension
   Exception Types:
Method:add
   Parameter Types: java.awt.Component java.lang.Object
   Returns:void
   Exception Types:
Method:remove
   Parameter Types: java.awt.MenuComponent
   Returns:void
   Exception Types:
Method:getLocation
   Parameter Types:
   Returns:java.awt.Point
   Exception Types:
Method:mouseDrag
   Parameter Types: java.awt.Event int int
   Returns:boolean
   Exception Types:
Method:checkImage
   Parameter Types: java.awt.Image java.awt.image.ImageObserver
   Returns:int
   Exception Types:
Method:printAll
   Parameter Types: java.awt.Graphics
```

```
                Returns:void
                Exception Types:
          Method:addComponentListener
                Parameter Types: java.awt.event.ComponentListener
                Returns:void
                Exception Types:
          Method:lostFocus
                Parameter Types: java.awt.Event java.lang.Object
                Returns:boolean
                Exception Types:
          Method:isAncestorOf
                Parameter Types: java.awt.Component
                Returns:boolean
                Exception Types:
          Method:getBounds
                Parameter Types:
                Returns:java.awt.Rectangle
                Exception Types:
          Method:isValid
                Parameter Types:
                Returns:boolean
                Exception Types:
          Method:action
                Parameter Types: java.awt.Event java.lang.Object
                Returns:boolean
                Exception Types:
          Method:doLayout
                Parameter Types:
                Returns:void
                Exception Types:
          Method:removeContainerListener
                Parameter Types: java.awt.event.ContainerListener
                Returns:void
                Exception Types:
          Method:paintComponents
                Parameter Types: java.awt.Graphics
                Returns:void
                Exception Types:
          Method:removeKeyListener
                Parameter Types: java.awt.event.KeyListener
                Returns:void
                Exception Types:
          Method:addFocusListener
                Parameter Types: java.awt.event.FocusListener
                Returns:void
```

```
   Exception Types:
Method:getParent
   Parameter Types:
   Returns:java.awt.Container
   Exception Types:
Method:requestFocus
   Parameter Types:
   Returns:void
   Exception Types:
Method:minimumSize
   Parameter Types:
   Returns:java.awt.Dimension
   Exception Types:
Method:bounds
   Parameter Types:
   Returns:java.awt.Rectangle
   Exception Types:
Method:getPreferredSize
   Parameter Types:
   Returns:java.awt.Dimension
   Exception Types:
Method:getLayout
   Parameter Types:
   Returns:java.awt.LayoutManager
   Exception Types:
Method:getMinimumSize
   Parameter Types:
   Returns:java.awt.Dimension
   Exception Types:
Method:add
   Parameter Types: java.awt.Component java.lang.Object int
   Returns:void
   Exception Types:
Method:getCursor
   Parameter Types:
   Returns:java.awt.Cursor
   Exception Types:
Method:getTreeLock
   Parameter Types:
   Returns:java.lang.Object
   Exception Types:
Method:mouseEnter
   Parameter Types: java.awt.Event int int
   Returns:boolean
   Exception Types:
```

```
Method: equals
   Parameter Types: java.lang.Object
   Returns: boolean
   Exception Types:
Method: setLocation
   Parameter Types: int int
   Returns: void
   Exception Types:
Method: remove
   Parameter Types: java.awt.Component
   Returns: void
   Exception Types:
Method: validate
   Parameter Types:
   Returns: void
   Exception Types:
Method: dispatchEvent
   Parameter Types: java.awt.AWTEvent
   Returns: void
   Exception Types:
Method: isEnabled
   Parameter Types:
   Returns: boolean
   Exception Types:
Method: setName
   Parameter Types: java.lang.String
   Returns: void
   Exception Types:
Method: layout
   Parameter Types:
   Returns: void
   Exception Types:
Method: mouseDown
   Parameter Types: java.awt.Event int int
   Returns: boolean
   Exception Types:
Method: getPeer
   Parameter Types:
   Returns: java.awt.peer.ComponentPeer
   Exception Types:
Method: list
   Parameter Types: java.io.PrintStream int
   Returns: void
   Exception Types:
Method: setCount
```

```
   Parameter Types: int
   Returns: void
   Exception Types:
Method: removeNotify
   Parameter Types:
   Returns: void
   Exception Types:
Method: getLocationOnScreen
   Parameter Types:
   Returns: java.awt.Point
   Exception Types:
Method: getGraphics
   Parameter Types:
   Returns: java.awt.Graphics
   Exception Types:
Method: getToolkit
   Parameter Types:
   Returns: java.awt.Toolkit
   Exception Types:
Method: countComponents
   Parameter Types:
   Returns: int
   Exception Types:
Method: mouseUp
   Parameter Types: java.awt.Event int int
   Returns: boolean
   Exception Types:
Method: removeComponentListener
   Parameter Types: java.awt.event.ComponentListener
   Returns: void
   Exception Types:
Method: setSize
   Parameter Types: java.awt.Dimension
   Returns: void
   Exception Types:
Method: getLocale
   Parameter Types:
   Returns: java.util.Locale
   Exception Types:
Method: notifyAll
   Parameter Types:
   Returns: void
   Exception Types:
Method: getClass
   Parameter Types:
```

```
        Returns:java.lang.Class
        Exception Types:
Method:getInsets
        Parameter Types:
        Returns:java.awt.Insets
        Exception Types:
Method:setSize
        Parameter Types: int int
        Returns:void
        Exception Types:
Method:paintAll
        Parameter Types: java.awt.Graphics
        Returns:void
        Exception Types:
Method:createImage
        Parameter Types: int int
        Returns:java.awt.Image
        Exception Types:
Method:transferFocus
        Parameter Types:
        Returns:void
        Exception Types:
Method:insets
        Parameter Types:
        Returns:java.awt.Insets
        Exception Types:
Method:invalidate
        Parameter Types:
        Returns:void
        Exception Types:
Method:getComponentCount
        Parameter Types:
        Returns:int
        Exception Types:
Method:inside
        Parameter Types: int int
        Returns:boolean
        Exception Types:
Method:getFont
        Parameter Types:
        Returns:java.awt.Font
        Exception Types:
Method:add
        Parameter Types: java.awt.Component int
        Returns:java.awt.Component
```

```
   Exception Types:
Method:getColorModel
   Parameter Types:
   Returns:java.awt.image.ColorModel
   Exception Types:
Method:move
   Parameter Types: int int
   Returns:void
   Exception Types:
Method:list
   Parameter Types: java.io.PrintStream
   Returns:void
   Exception Types:
Method:update
   Parameter Types: java.awt.Graphics
   Returns:void
   Exception Types:
Method:handleEvent
   Parameter Types: java.awt.Event
   Returns:boolean
   Exception Types:
Method:getComponents
   Parameter Types:
   Returns:[Ljava.awt.Component;
   Exception Types:
Method:preferredSize
   Parameter Types:
   Returns:java.awt.Dimension
   Exception Types:
Method:getComponentAt
   Parameter Types: java.awt.Point
   Returns:java.awt.Component
   Exception Types:
Method:setVisible
   Parameter Types: boolean
   Returns:void
   Exception Types:
Method:addKeyListener
   Parameter Types: java.awt.event.KeyListener
   Returns:void
   Exception Types:
Method:contains
   Parameter Types: int int
   Returns:boolean
   Exception Types:
```

```
Method:mouseExit
   Parameter Types: java.awt.Event int int
   Returns:boolean
   Exception Types:
Method:toString
   Parameter Types:
   Returns:java.lang.String
   Exception Types:
Method:repaint
   Parameter Types: long int int int int
   Returns:void
   Exception Types:
Method:remove
   Parameter Types: int
   Returns:void
   Exception Types:
Method:getComponent
   Parameter Types: int
   Returns:java.awt.Component
   Exception Types:
Method:cycleCount
   Parameter Types:
   Returns:void
   Exception Types:
Method:list
   Parameter Types: java.io.PrintWriter
   Returns:void
   Exception Types:
Method:reshape
   Parameter Types: int int int int
   Returns:void
   Exception Types:
Method:getBackground
   Parameter Types:
   Returns:java.awt.Color
   Exception Types:
Method:getMaximumSize
   Parameter Types:
   Returns:java.awt.Dimension
   Exception Types:
Method:contains
   Parameter Types: java.awt.Point
   Returns:boolean
   Exception Types:
Method:repaint
```

```
      Parameter Types: long
      Returns: void
      Exception Types:
Method: checkImage
      Parameter Types: java.awt.Image int int java.awt.image.ImageObserver
      Returns: int
      Exception Types:
Method: gotFocus
      Parameter Types: java.awt.Event java.lang.Object
      Returns: boolean
      Exception Types:
Method: removeMouseMotionListener
      Parameter Types: java.awt.event.MouseMotionListener
      Returns: void
      Exception Types:
Method: resize
      Parameter Types: int int
      Returns: void
      Exception Types:
Method: removeMouseListener
      Parameter Types: java.awt.event.MouseListener
      Returns: void
      Exception Types:
Method: isShowing
      Parameter Types:
      Returns: boolean
      Exception Types:
Method: disable
      Parameter Types:
      Returns: void
      Exception Types:
Method: paint
      Parameter Types: java.awt.Graphics
      Returns: void
      Exception Types:
Method: addMouseListener
      Parameter Types: java.awt.event.MouseListener
      Returns: void
      Exception Types:
Method: setLocation
      Parameter Types: java.awt.Point
      Returns: void
      Exception Types:
Method: show
      Parameter Types: boolean
```

```
        Returns:void
        Exception Types:
Method:setBounds
        Parameter Types: int int int int
        Returns:void
        Exception Types:
Method:getForeground
        Parameter Types:
        Returns:java.awt.Color
        Exception Types:
Method:removeAll
        Parameter Types:
        Returns:void
        Exception Types:
Method:prepareImage
        Parameter Types: java.awt.Image int int java.awt.image.ImageObserver
        Returns:boolean
        Exception Types:
Method:printComponents
        Parameter Types: java.awt.Graphics
        Returns:void
        Exception Types:
Method:getComponentAt
        Parameter Types: int int
        Returns:java.awt.Component
        Exception Types:
Method:wait
        Parameter Types: long int
        Returns:void
        Exception Types: java.lang.InterruptedException
Method:keyDown
        Parameter Types: java.awt.Event int
        Returns:boolean
        Exception Types:
Method:add
        Parameter Types: java.awt.PopupMenu
        Returns:void
        Exception Types:
Method:setFont
        Parameter Types: java.awt.Font
        Returns:void
        Exception Types:
Method:setLayout
        Parameter Types: java.awt.LayoutManager
        Returns:void
```

```
   Exception Types:
Method:setCursor
   Parameter Types: java.awt.Cursor
   Returns:void
   Exception Types:
Method:setBackground
   Parameter Types: java.awt.Color
   Returns:void
   Exception Types:
Method:mouseMove
   Parameter Types: java.awt.Event int int
   Returns:boolean
   Exception Types:
Method:hide
   Parameter Types:
   Returns:void
   Exception Types:
Method:getCount
   Parameter Types:
   Returns:int
   Exception Types:
Method:print
   Parameter Types: java.awt.Graphics
   Returns:void
   Exception Types:
Method:getFontMetrics
   Parameter Types: java.awt.Font
   Returns:java.awt.FontMetrics
   Exception Types:
Method:addMouseMotionListener
   Parameter Types: java.awt.event.MouseMotionListener
   Returns:void
   Exception Types:
Method:repaint
   Parameter Types: int int int int
   Returns:void
   Exception Types:
Method:deliverEvent
   Parameter Types: java.awt.Event
   Returns:void
   Exception Types:
Method:resize
   Parameter Types: java.awt.Dimension
   Returns:void
   Exception Types:
```

```
Method:setEnabled
   Parameter Types: boolean
   Returns:void
   Exception Types:
Method:removeFocusListener
   Parameter Types: java.awt.event.FocusListener
   Returns:void
   Exception Types:
Method:notify
   Parameter Types:
   Returns:void
   Exception Types:
Method:setForeground
   Parameter Types: java.awt.Color
   Returns:void
   Exception Types:
Method:nextFocus
   Parameter Types:
   Returns:void
   Exception Types:
Method:postEvent
   Parameter Types: java.awt.Event
   Returns:boolean
   Exception Types:
Method:keyUp
   Parameter Types: java.awt.Event int
   Returns:boolean
   Exception Types:
Method:add
   Parameter Types: java.awt.Component
   Returns:java.awt.Component
   Exception Types:
Method:setBounds
   Parameter Types: java.awt.Rectangle
   Returns:void
   Exception Types:
Method:hashCode
   Parameter Types:
   Returns:int
   Exception Types:
Method:add
   Parameter Types: java.lang.String java.awt.Component
   Returns:java.awt.Component
   Exception Types:
Method:list
```

```
   Parameter Types: java.io.PrintWriter int
   Returns:void
   Exception Types:
Method:getName
   Parameter Types:
   Returns:java.lang.String
   Exception Types:
Method:imageUpdate
   Parameter Types: java.awt.Image int int int int int
   Returns:boolean
   Exception Types:
Method:setLocale
   Parameter Types: java.util.Locale
   Returns:void
   Exception Types:
Method:getAlignmentY
   Parameter Types:
   Returns:float
   Exception Types:
Method:getAlignmentX
   Parameter Types:
   Returns:float
   Exception Types:
Method:prepareImage
   Parameter Types: java.awt.Image java.awt.image.ImageObserver
   Returns:boolean
   Exception Types:
Method:wait
   Parameter Types: long
   Returns:void
   Exception Types: java.lang.InterruptedException
```

Index

access methods, 32
addExplosionEventListener, 53
addPetesEventListener, 53
addPropertyChangeListener, 46, 48, 156
addVetoableChangeListener, 49
AlphaBeatEvent, 187
Applet1, 19
attributeNames, 113

backgroundProperty, 49
BDK, 16
Bean Development Kit (BDK), 16
BeanBox, 16, 175
BeanDescriptor, 15, 110, 114, 119, 148
BeanInfo, 4, 14, 18, 109, 110, 119–121, 124, 137, 144, 145, 201
Beans, 2
before, 107
BetaBeatEvent, 188
bi.getPropertyDescriptors(), 125
BIExBeanInfo, 122
bit rot, 68

BoingPanel1, 183, 189
boolean, 132

Calendar, 90
CartPanel1, 183, 192
CharacterIterator, 91
CHINA, 93
ChoiceFormat, 106
Class, 18, 131–133, 138
ClassNotFoundException, 60, 66
ColorOutOfFashionEvent, 79, 80
Constructor, 131, 134, 144
core reflection, 109
customization, 7
Customizer, 15

DataInput, 60, 61
DataInputStream, 60
DataOutput, 60, 61, 71
DateFormat, 90
DateFormatData, 90
decapitalize, 120
DecimalFormat, 103–105
DecimalFormatSymbol, 104, 105
defaultReadObject, 62, 65, 70
defaultWriteObject, 62, 70
design patterns, 8, 40

219

design signature, 8, 40
DisplayCompilerErrorEvent,
        76
DisplayCompilerMessageEvent,
        76
DisplayCompilerWarningEvent,
        76
displayName, 113
DogPanel1, 183, 195
doGreen, 28
doRed, 28, 35
double, 106, 132
doYellow, 28

Enumeration, 94, 113
equal, 143
event, 75
event adapter, 77, 85, 169
event loop, 75
Event SetDescriptor, 110
EventListener, 53, 76, 78
EventObject, 27, 37, 76, 86
events, 7
EventSetDescriptor, 111, 114,
        117, 118
ExplosionEventListener, 53
Externalizable, 62, 71

fattenPath, 123
FeatureDescriptor, 110–112,
        114, 117, 119
Field, 18, 131, 137, 143
FileOutputStream, 100
firePropertyChange, 46, 49
fireVetoableChange, 49
FontMetrics, 91
format, 101, 103
Format, 106

forName(String), 132
Fruit, 157
FruitEditor, 157

get, 139
getAdditionalBeanInfo, 111
getAddListenerMethod, 118
getAsText, 154
getAvailableLocales, 103
getBeanClass, 119
getBeanCustomizer, 119
getBeanDescriptor, 110, 122
getBeanInfo, 110, 119–121,
        201
getBeanInfoSearchPath, 120
getBoolean, 137
getBundle, 97
getByte, 137
getChar, 137
getClass, 131
getComponentType, 133
getConstructors, 134
getContents, 98, 99
getContructor(Class[]), 134
getCurrencyInstance, 103
getCustomEditor, 156
getDecimalFormatSymbol,
        104
getDeclaredConstructors(Class[]),134
getDeclaredConstructor,134
getDeclaredField(String), 133
getDeclaredMethod(String,
        Class[]), 134
getDeclaredMethods(), 134
getDeclaringClass, 138, 143
getDefault, 97

getDefaultEventIndex, 111
getDefaultPropertyIndex, 111,
        122
getDisplayName, 112
getDouble, 137
getEventSetDescriptors,   110,
        122
getExceptionTypes, 143
getFields, 133, 137
getFloat, 137
getIcon, 112
getIndexedPropertyType, 117
getIndexedReadMethod, 117
getIndexedWriteMethod, 117
getInstance, 103, 106
getInt, 137, 139
getInterfaces, 133, 183
getJavaInitializationString,
        156
getKeys, 94
getListenerMethodDescriptors,
        117
getListenerMethods, 117
getListenerType, 117
getLocale, 22, 108
getLong, 137
getMethod, 114
getMethod(String,   Class[]),
        134
getMethodDescriptors,   111,
        122
getMethods(), 134
getModifiers, 135, 143
getName, 112, 131, 132, 143
getNewValue, 49, 171
getNumberInstance, 103
getObject, 96

getOldValue, 49
getParameterDescriptors, 115
getParameterTypes, 144
getPercentInstance, 103
getPropertyDescriptors,   111,
        122, 125
getPropertyEditorClass, 116
getPropertyName, 49
getPropertyType, 115
getReadMethod, 116
getRemoveListenerMethod,
        118
getResourceBundle, 99
getReturnType, 144
getShortDescription, 113
getSigners, 132
getString, 96
getStringArray, 96
getSuperclass, 132, 135
getTags, 154, 157
getValue, 113, 155
getWriteMethod, 116, 117
goGreen, 175
goRed, 175
goYellow, 175
granularity, 5
Graphics, 155
GregorianCalendar, 90, 107

handleGetObject, 94
Hashtable, 93, 100

ICON_COLOR_16x16, 112
ICON_COLOR_32x32, 112
ICON_MONO_16x16, 112
ICON_MONO_32x32, 112
IllegalAccessException,   135,
        137, 138

IllegalArgumentException,
        137–139, 154
IndexedPropertyDescriptor,
        116
InputEvent, 82
instanceof, 133
instantiate, 20, 177
int, 132
Integer, 61
internationalization, 10
Internationalization API, 89
introspection, 6, 28, 109
Introspector, 120, 124
InvalidObjectException, 66
invoke, 114
invoke(Object,Object[]), 144
isAbstract, 138
isArray, 132
isAssignableFrom(Class), 133
isBound, 116
isConstrained, 116
isExpert, 113
isFinal, 138
isHidden, 113
isInDefaultEventSet, 118
isInstance(Object), 133
isInterface, 132
ISO-3166, 92
ISO-639, 92
isPaintable, 155
isPrimitive, 132
isProtected, 138
isPublic, 138
isStatic, 138
isSynchronized, 138
isTransient, 138
isUnicast, 118

isVolatile, 138

JAR file, 160
java.lang.reflect, 131
java.util.EventObject, 78

KeyEvent, 75
KEY_RELEASE, 75

Label, 169
lightState, 31
ListenerList, 177
ListResourceBundle, 97–99
Locale, 22, 91, 97, 103

Member, 131, 143, 145
MessageFormat, 102, 106
Method, 18, 114–117, 131, 143
MethodDescriptor, 111, 114,
        117, 119, 201
Modifiers, 138
MouseEvent, 75, 82
MOUSE_DRAG, 75
MOUSE_UP, 75
multicast, 84
MyClass, 110
MyClassBeanInfo, 110

new, 177
newInstance, 135
NewLightEvent, 19, 25, 27, 31
NewLightEventListener, 27,
        31, 35
NoSuchFieldException, 135
NoSuchMethodException, 135
NotActiveException, 63
NumBean, 169
NumberFormat, 90, 93, 102,
        103, 106

NumberFormatData, 90

Object, 131
object validation, 66
ObjectInput, 60, 71
ObjectInputStream, 60–62, 68
ObjectInputValidation, 68
ObjectOutput, 60, 61, 71
ObjectOutputStream, 60–63

paintValue, 155, 157
Panel, 31
ParameterDescriptor, 111, 115, 201
parse, 102
persistence, 9
PetesEventListener, 53
plumbFields, 139
properties, 8, 41
Properties, 93, 100
property editors, 8
propertyChange, 46, 48, 49, 171
PropertyChangeEvent, 15, 48, 153, 169–171, 175
PropertyChangeEvents, 54, 155
PropertyChangeListener, 16, 47–49, 51, 157, 171
PropertyChangeSupport, 46, 48
PropertyDescriptor, 111, 114–117, 122, 130
PropertyEditor, 15, 153, 154
PropertyResourceBundle, 99, 100
PropertyVetoException, 50, 51, 163

readExternal, 71
readObject, 59–61, 63, 65, 179
registerValidation, 68
removeExplosionEventListener, 53
removePetesEventListener, 53
removePropertyChangeListener, 46, 48, 156
removeVetoableChangeListener, 49
ResourceBundle, 89, 91, 94, 97, 108

SecurityException, 135
serializable, 9
Serializable, 56, 72
set, 138
setAsText, 154, 155, 157
setBackgroundProperty, 51
setBeanInfoSearchPath, 121
setBoolean, 138
setBound, 116
setByte, 138
setChar, 137, 138
setConstrained, 116
setDecimalFormatSymbol, 104
setDecimalSeparator, 105
setDigit, 105
setDisplayName, 113
setDouble, 138
setExpert, 113
setFloat, 138
setGroupingSeparator, 105
setGroupingSize, 104, 105
setHidden, 113
setInDefaultEventSet, 118
setInfinity, 105

setInt, 138
setLong, 138
setMaximumFractionDigits,
        103
setMaximumIntegerDigits,
        103
setMinimumFractionDigits,
        103
setMinimumIntegerDigits, 103
setMinusSign, 105
setMultiplier, 104
setName], 112
setNaN, 105
setNegativePrefix, 104
setNegativeSuffix, 104
setPatternSeparator, 105
setPercentage, 105
setPerMill, 105
setPositivePrefix, 104
setPositiveSuffix, 104
setPropertyEditorClass, 116
setShortDescription, 113
setUnicast, 118
setValue, 113, 155
setZeroDigit, 105
SimpleBeanInfo, 122
SimpleDateFormat, 90
SimpleTimeZone, 90
someRandomObject, 61
static, 58
StopLightPanel, 19, 28
StringCharacterInterator, 91
supportsCustomEditor, 156

tellWhom, 177
TextBoundary, 91
ThermBean, 169

TimeZone, 90
TooManyListenersException,
        53, 84
toString, 101, 131, 132, 138
transient, 58
TreeApp, 184
TriPanel1, 183, 197

unicast, 84

validateObject, 62, 66
variant, 92
vetoableChange, 52
VetoableChangeListener,   49,
        51, 52, 163
VetoableChangeSupport, 49

WarnAdaptor, 169, 175
WarnBean, 169, 175, 176
WarnEvent, 173
writeChar, 60
writeDouble, 60
writeExternal, 71
writeObject,   20, 59–63, 72,
        179

yourFavoriteClass, 61